PRAISE FOR CONNECTION YOU!

"Connection is the breeding ground for success, and nobody speaks or writes about it better than the master connector, Sheila Stabile. Savor every word!!"

— Mikki Williams, Hall of Fame Speaker, TEDx, Executive Speech Coach, Creator of Speakers School and Keynote Kamp

"Sheila Stabile is a global expert in the art and power of connection—and this book will inspire and transform the way you look at connection with yourself, your family, your friends, your work, and your life."

— David Morey, Bestselling Author and Chairman, DMG Global

"It is counterintuitive; we are living in a world where people connect through social media in unprecedented ways, and yet... many still lack meaningful personal connections. Sheila K. Stabile's very fine book, ConnectionYou, *is thoughtful, practical, and helpful to all who will take the time to consider her perceptive advice. Read it and joyfully reconnect with who you are, others around you, and the world at large!"*

— John C. Bowling, President, Olivet Nazarene University

"Sheila is an amazing connector of individuals. Her ability to meet people where they are and to facilitate their awareness, knowledge, and skills is uncanny, and to that end, she possesses the unique ability to serve diverse audiences equally as well."

— Paul Harris, Ph.D., Assistant Professor,
University of Virginia

"Any organization that relies on a 'customer' base needs to relate to the people who make up that base to attract and retain them as customers or as members, in our case. This is true not only at the organizational level but especially at the personal level."

— Kwok-Sze Wong, EdD, Executive Director,
American School Counselor Association

CONNECTION YOU!

Build, Strengthen, and Profit
by Making Connections in Work,
Life, and Self

SHEILA K. STABILE

ISBN 978-1-936961-48-1

Books are available for special promotions and premiums.

For details, contact:

Special Markets
LINX Corp.
Box 613
Great Falls, VA 22066
Email specialmarkets@linxcorp.com

Published by LINX

LINX, Corp.
Box 613
Great Falls, VA 22066

www.linxcorp.com

Printed in the United States of America

BOOK DEDICATION

— Spencer and Max —

Connected from birth and forever to my heart.

Love, Mom

TABLE OF CONTENTS

PART 2: CONNECTION IN LIFE

PART 3: CONNECTION WITH SELF

RESOURCES

FOREWORD

Connections between people start with sharing and finding something in common, such as an experience, an acquaintance, a place where both people visited or live. This can lead to a deeper intellectual and emotional connection, understanding another beyond the shared commonalities. This is an understanding not only of the other person's character traits, and the history and culture behind those traits, but understanding that we can have a connection with another person even though we may not share the same culture, beliefs, or even preferences. Too often, people tend to relate only with people who look, act, or feel just like them. People who have a connection use what they share in common to bridge what they don't have in common.

I had just started my job as the executive director of the American School Counselor Association (ASCA). One of my responsibilities was to write a column for ASCA's magazine. Most executive directors highlight the articles in the magazine or provide some insight to the profession or current issues. I didn't want just to summarize the contents of the magazine. I wanted my column to be more meaningful, but I didn't want it to become too pedantic or didactic, as if I was all-knowing and the readers must hang on my every word. So, I wrote a story about my daughter in my first column. And I wrote about her in my second column. I didn't know it then, but I had stumbled on the key to connecting with ASCA members. Eventually, I wrote about my two sons as well. For almost twenty years, I've written a story about one of my children in every issue of the magazine, chronicling their changing interests, transitions through the different stages of their lives, their challenges and triumphs. ASCA members constantly tell me how much they appreciate and enjoy my columns. They feel like they know my children and have watched them grow up, even though they've never met them. And they feel like they know me, even when they've never met me. I realized that writing about my children was the way I could establish a connection with my members, who work with children and adolescents. By connecting with my children, ASCA members connected with me as a parent, and ultimately with me as the executive director of their professional association. I believe this connection has been crucial to ASCA's success and to my effectiveness as executive director.

I've learned many lessons from writing my column through the years. First, I've learned solutions come when you least expect them, and even when you don't know you have a problem. I didn't think my column was particularly problematic, but it's become one of the most important ways we help ASCA members feel they are a part of the association.

Second, I've learned it is possible to establish a relationship with a large number of people you've never met. Politicians and leaders do it all the time. I never thought it was possible—or even necessary—in my job as executive director to establish a connection with more than 30,000 people, many of whom I'll never meet personally, but I do feel a connection with most of them. And more importantly, when I meet them, it's apparent they feel a connection with me.

Finally, I've learned that making a connection is important when you're trying to establish a relationship with people. Any organization that relies on a "customer" base needs to relate to the people who make up that base to attract and retain them as customers or as members in our case. This is true not only at the organizational level but especially at the personal level.

Kwok-Sze Wong, EdD
Executive Director
American School Counselor Association

MY FASCINATION
WITH CONNECTION

I have always been fascinated with people—what drives them, what they have accomplished or their journey to do so, how they think and view the world. Each little piece of another person has formed and continues to form me in ways that I view and experience the world. Increasingly, I experience how we are connected and how we all need to take care of each other for deeper connection.

As a schoolteacher, it was fascinating to observe the variety of ways my students learned through various learning styles: visually, aurally, or kinesthetically. It was important to use different learning styles to understand those differences in maximizing their connection to learning and performing.

As a salesperson, these lessons continued. It was important to bring a personal touch to my selling and understand the behavioral styles of my customers. Selling was not only about closing but building trust and tailoring my selling to connect to each of them. Finding ways to show them

I cared by finding out what they were thinking, asking the right questions, and leading from the heart increased the connection.

While a business development manager, my primary tasks were looking for new ways to initiate business and build long-term relationships with prospects to increase company revenue. This required engaging with the people we wanted to do business with, demonstrating interest, and learning about them. Although this sounds straightforward, it required listening, caring, and strategy. It required intentional connection. In some ways, it was like being back in my classroom, learning all the ways the students responded and connecting at an emotional level.

As a volunteer, my goal is always to build trust and offer ideation. I want my volunteering to exhibit how I do business. Listening, caring, and looking to find common ground for that connection that serving creates. Give and take—that balance is critical. How you do anything is how you do everything.

Connection has always been at the height of my curiosity. The need for richer connection and inclusion is fundamental.

I have observed first-hand the dangers of a person losing connection with the outside world. The results of rejection, depression, isolation, loneliness, and anger resulted in great pain and suffering for this person.

MY FASCINATION WITH CONNECTION

Research shows that social support wards off the effects of depression and other health problems. Simply starting to say "hello" to those you encounter each day, being intentional and offering a smile, or a simple acknowledgment of another's existence is a step toward real-life changes.

The art and science of connection is powerful with others, ourselves, and in business. It's contagious. Sparking, initiating, and maintaining connections can increase profits, create more happiness, abundance, and well-being, and even more powerfully—they can save lives.

Here's to richer connecting,
Sheila

PART 1
CONNECTION AT WORK

INTRODUCTION

*I used to want to fix people, but now
I just want to be with them.*
— Bob Goff, author, *Love Does*

The power of connection in the workplace is one of the most powerful advantages a company can cultivate. It allows employees to become more productive and have a better sense of well-being, which translates into increased health and happiness.

We live in a world where most of our workweek is spent using technology. Although this has allowed us to communicate better with tools like graphs, outlines, online shopping, search engines, and software, communication that was once between employees has now changed to looking at screens via phones and computers.

The heart of leadership is connection and caring. It takes a team to encourage each other; we can't do it alone. Hearing affirmations that we are doing a good job or the encouragement that we can do a good job is important to all of us. Connection in the workplace can give people more energy and ignite creativity, whereas the cost of not connecting affects personal health, loyalty, and the company's bottom line.

In the Society for Human Resource Management's (SHRM's) 2016 Employee Job Satisfaction and Engagement Report, relationships with fellow workers were a top driver of employee engagement, and 77 percent of those taking the assessment listed connections as a priority. Gallup estimates that low connectivity costs the U.S. between $450 billion and $550 billion in poor productivity, profit loss, and attrition.

Fostering connection is a learnable skill that can be nurtured and developed. Leaders should consider promoting connection as a focus in their work. Employees should evaluate where they can begin to develop relationships. Getting to know team members and sharing experiences together allows for connection in a powerful way. Salespeople can implement relation-centered connections with their customers.

Connection in the workplace takes intention, and it's never too late! Perhaps Simon Sinek said it best: "Being connected is not the same as connecting. Our survival is based on community." Just love people! It is a great leadership, customer service, and team-building principle. When you focus on loving and connecting in the workplace, your business will grow. One person at a time can create a ripple effect that builds a better company and surrounds the people around you with value. When people feel connected to both their team and their company's mission, the benefits are huge.

1. A WAY WITH WORDS

While I nodded, nearly napping,
suddenly there came a tapping . . .

— Edgar Allan Poe, "The Raven"

Alliteration is the repetition of sounds at the beginnings of words or in stressed syllables. Companies use this alliterative technique all the time to make sure that their brand names are memorable. I've been thinking about alliteration in business lately and how it can increase connection. Consider, for example, some of the well-known companies that have used alliteration in their names: Bed Bath & Beyond, Dunkin' Donuts, and American Airlines. Additionally, names that use alliteration help make them more memorable. Fictional names such as Mickey Mouse, Donald Duck, and SpongeBob SquarePants, as well as real people like Marilyn Monroe, Jessie Jackson, and Ronald Reagan, stick in my head.

Thus, alliteration has an adhering effect and "sticks" and binds to us like glue. We can create alliteration in our business interactions for a sense of fun, whimsy, and greater personal connection, as well as deepening team engagement.

Consider in your company or team:

- *Make It Happen Monday*—What goal could you set for a great tone for the week?
- *Tidbit Tuesday*—Create a board or gathering place where the team can share something interesting to give others good ideas.
- *Wishful Wednesday*—What is something you wish your team could do?
- *Thoughtful Thursday*—Can the team or company contribute needed community-minded actions?
- *Funny Friday*—Since everyone loves sharing a good joke, this can be a great lift-off to the weekend and feeling good about the company.

Whenever and wherever you can add a spark of excitement, you can reengage your team. It creates interaction.

Who does not like alliteration?

A way with words will work wonders and add wit and wisdom to your workplace. It "wheely" does!

|································|

Add alliteration to your team activities to make them memorable and fun.

2. EVERYONE MATTERS

Paychecks can't buy passion.

— Brad Federman, human resource consultant

Never discount the value and connection that an employee can offer.

Antonio is the bellman at a hotel on Michigan Avenue in downtown Chicago. His smile and energy instantly confirms that you have arrived at the perfect hotel for your trip. Antonio is the face—specifically the eyes and ears—of the hotel. He greets the guests, sees the street activity, and is a keen observer of the traffic in and out of the hotel, as well as the area outside of it.

Upon a break, his intriguing aura motivated me to have a conversation with him. During our exchange, a woman passed and greeted him as she walked into the hotel. He informed me she was simply passing in and out to obtain a copy of the *Financial Times*. She knew him and he knew her. It was routine and part of the daily landscape.

CONNECTION YOU!

A Chicago police car pulled up along the curb for a few moments and chatted with Antonio. Not business—just pleasure, community, attachment, and kinship.

Antonio loves his job. He loves the company. He was on a billboard and featured in business magazines as the face of the company. His contagious energy is the best marketing this hotel chain could possibly maintain. He generates a connection that is priceless.

Identifying influencers in your organization and investing in the training to allow them to understand your brand is one of the best investments a company can make. Providing employees with the tools to communicate the brand and build excitement will extend the impact of the company. It allows loyalty to be created for the company and enhances the well-being of the individual and company. Everyone matters, every role matters.

|································|

*Appreciate how impactful each position
in a company is to your business.*

3. MMM MMM GOOD TOUCHPOINTS

The time to build a network is always before you need one.
— Douglas Conant, American businessman

The Campbell Soup Company holds a special place in American culture with their clever slogan of "Mmm Mmm Good!" Artist Andy Warhol painted the bright red can, which made its way into pop culture.

What is also "souper" and delicious about this company is that when employee engagement was down, they hired a new CEO, Douglas Conant. He was able to lead the company through five years of consistent growth. He implemented the Campbell Success Model. His philosophy of using incidental interactions, and connecting with employees in personal ways, ignited enthusiasm within the company, resulting in higher employee engagement, improved growth and revenue, and better customer relationships.

Some of his implementations included:

- Wearing a pedometer, with a goal of 10,000 steps a day, to physically interact with as many employees personally each day as possible.
- Writing personal handwritten notes to employees, noting specific contributions.
- Using interruptions as an opportunity for "touchpoints" to share the company's mission, values, purpose, and agenda.

Mr. Conant coauthored a book with Mette Norgaard called *Touchpoints: Creating Powerful Leadership Connections in the Smallest of Moments.*

The concept of making a business "mmm mmm good" requires heart-centered leadership. Heart-centered leadership creates connection. Connection increases the return on investment (ROI) and the well-being of each employee.

Integrity is listed as the number-one character issue for leadership in America.

Leading with the mindset of people, people, people and embracing relationships contributes to everyone's success both personally and professionally. It has been said that building a reputation of integrity take years, but only a second to lose.

|································|

Consider what touchpoints you can implement in your company and life interactions for deeper connection.

4. BONDING THROUGH TEAM BUILDING

Everybody wants a friendly work environment, where people are comfortable and happy to talk to and work with anyone.

Cohesiveness is an important factor in implementing effective, high-performance teams. It is the ability to get team members inspired. Understanding how team cohesiveness works and how team bonding will build energy and connectedness is powerful. True ROI is inspiring your team members through reinforcing their sense of belonging, empathy in bonding, mutual respect, and keeping humor in your workplace. Bonding with your team can be a simple and inexpensive adventure that has strong sticking power.

|······························|

Try team-building games to get your team to connect and work together better.

5. AN HONEST TEA-RIFFIC CONNECTION

Believe in what you are doing. You have to have a passion for it.

—Seth Goldman, businessman

Honest Tea was the top-selling organic tea in the United States in 2017. In a recent meeting I attended at the National Association of Business Owners and Entrepreneurs, Seth Goldman, Honest Tea's cofounder, shared thoughts about their mission, values, and profitability. The word "honest" immediately creates a bond.

I had the opportunity to ask Seth a few questions.

Q: What do you think "honest" means in your name?

Seth: It means you are going to do what you said you would do. It's an authentic connection to nature and people all around the world. Growth and innovation need to be interwoven. It immediately creates a bond.

CONNECTION YOU!

Q: What made you invent Honest Tea?

Seth: I wanted to create a healthy drink for my runs, but I also wanted to create something healthy for the planet and available for everyone, not just those who could afford it. I learned by drinking tea with other people all over the world that friendships were formed and it connected people and nature.

Q: What was your philosophy of a start-up venture?

Seth: A need for vision, communicating and connecting to your team, and giving the resources to my team. The marketplace funds the tea, so we needed to make something attractive for the social and financial return.

Honest Tea connects, too, with their suppliers, as they purchase their sugar and teas to gain the Fair-Trade Certification that help fund community development projects such as schools, industrial farming equipment, and ambulances.

Seth shared a story with the audience, in which they'd given the consumer the chance to be honest. They developed a social experiment to find out if people would pay for their beverages on the honor system (without anyone watching) at unattended kiosks around the country. The results were fascinating and proved the transparent connection, reinforcing that overall people were honest. (results can be read at www.NationalHonestyIndex.com).

5. AN HONEST TEA-RIFFIC CONNECTION

Honest Tea's success is attributed to their creation of a mission-driven company with their connection and commitment to "Communi-Tea."

|································|

Develop strong and deep relationships to your brand by always returning to your mission.

6. "I NEED YOUR HELP." ASK!

Learn to be an askhole.

—Jack Canfield, author, *Success Principles* and
coauthor, *Chicken Soup for the Soul*

If you don't ask, the answer is always no. If you ask and the answer is yes, you have a new connection.

Asking for help is one of the greatest skills that successful people learn to do well and that will save you time and money. When I was transitioning from a sales executive to a business development manager, the environment was a 360-degree turn for me. My assignment was to increase the client base, add more prospects to the pipeline and, as my manager stated, "Shake it up!"

It took risk, strategy, and background work on the prospects. I was specific in whom I asked. The most significant lesson I learned was to simply state, "I need your help." Being vulnerable was not easy; however, it produced results. People want to help you if you are prepared, personable, and genuine (not a mass email). Together, this is a recipe for connection and proved very beneficial to me in creating new business connections.

My recipe was to research for the right potential prospects, learning as much about them as I could, what I wanted them to help me with, and give them information about me and my goal. I always included, "I need or would love your help."

This fascination led me to become a certified trainer in Jack Canfield's Success Principles.

In his book *The Aladdin Factor*, Jack Canfield offers these tips to get you started:

1. Ask as if you expect it.
2. Assume you can.
3. Ask someone who can give it to you.
4. Be clear and specific.

Asking for help initially requires short-term discomfort for a long-term benefit. Remember to always say thank-you!

|································|

Be vulnerable—start asking for help today.

7. MAKE IT EASY

All things are difficult before they are easy.
—Thomas Fuller, English historian

As a sales representative for several years at a Fortune 500 company, a key to success was making it easy for the customer to understand the ordering and procurement processes. When customers are comfortable and you make their lives less complex, it allows them to maintain business with you and prevents them from going to a competitor. As a sales representative, being ready to serve and making it easy for the customer keeps them connected to you. It sets you up for success.

Put your consumer hat on. Think about the companies that you enjoy doing business with because they make your life easier. Nordstrom's, which puts a tag on each item purchased so a return can easily be scanned to get the original purchase information. There is no need to worry about digging up a receipt. Amazon keeps all ordering information loaded with free shipping from Prime so it is simple to reorder. They maintain any address you have shipped to, thus reducing the need to re-enter information. Their return policy is seamless and all forms are ready for you.

Likewise, I made it easy on my customers by providing ready-made custom order forms so there was no need to look up codes for products. I supplied magnets with all the numbers they would need to make orders or get customer service so they would not have to search where to get their information. I set up training sessions with all those involved in purchasing for the ordering process to make it easier for their routine ordering. Additionally, I would bring in vendor representatives to discuss products that would be helpful in various areas of the company. Working with my inside sales team to make them aware of the special needs of my customers or key contacts if there were any challenges was an additional way to making it personal and increase the connection. The combination of making it easy and setting up these connections inside and outside the company created convenience and customer loyalty.

We are all busy. We have many choices about where to buy products, who to support, and who to go to when we need something unique or perhaps quickly. Be ahead of the game by adding value and consistently making it easy for your customer processes. When it is time to buy, they will remember you. Consider how this could work in your business or sales situation and what you

7. MAKE IT EASY

could implement to make a process easier for your customer base.

|······························|

Make it easy for customers to buy from you and they will stay connected.

8. MORE FUN
ON SALES CALLS

Creativity is intelligence having fun.

—Albert Einstein, Theoretical physicist

For many salespeople like myself, making initial sales calls sometimes can be as apprehensive as going to the dentist. You know you need to do it, you want the end result; however, the anticipation is unnerving. You wonder if they will say no, hang up, or give you the cold shoulder.

I learned a few tricks that kept me motivated, kept it fun, and moved me closer to connecting to customers accepting my calls and moving them closer to meeting with me.

Here are a few things to create a positive mindset when connecting with potential customers:

1. Play some upbeat music. If I was working from the home office, I would play some tunes that put me in a happy mood and sometimes had me tapping my

feet. If I had to travel a few miles to my prospect or customer, the radio would be on during the travel. Music helps create a positive mindset.

2. Visualize your customer. Your customer has many people calling, and if you can create a mental picture of them working at their desk with piles of papers around them, your empathy will be increased. Reverse the scenario: you are busy, you get a call, you want the person on the other end of the phone to get to the point. If that were you and someone wanted your business, what could you say and do to deliver a powerful message and be respectful of their busy moment?

3. Have a unique line ready. If it is a customer who has not purchased from you before and you are trying to make a connection, think of something "outside the box" to move them emotionally closer to you. It is helpful to study and research the customer ahead of time to make this relatable and powerful. Willie was a prospect whom I had not been successful with getting in the door. On my next phone call to him, I said, "Willie, this is Sheila. I was wondering what color tie you are wearing today." He seemed stunned. "What, I don't have a tie on." I responded, "Well, if you did have a tie on, what color do you think it would be today?" After laughing, we were able to begin a conversation that resulted in setting up an initial meeting. And I got the sale!

8. MORE FUN ON SALES CALLS

Think "outside the box" to get in the door and to connect, which enables you to build the relationship with your customer. Ponder what you can do in your environment to set the stage. Visualize your prospect on the other end of the phone and how you can fit into their scenario for the fastest connection.

|·······························|

Play music and visualize your customer to set the stage for energetic sales calls.

9. BEST FRIEND IN THE WORKPLACE

"We'll be friends forever, won't we, Pooh?" asked Piglet.
"Even longer," Pooh answered.
—A.A. Milne, author, *Winnie-the-Pooh*

Having quality relationships and friendships is a very important part of a healthy workplace. The Gallup organization has found that a key trait of employee retention is to develop trusting relationships.

As a Gallup certified strength coach, I often get asked about question number ten on the Clifton assessment.

The item, "I have a best friend at work," is clearly one of the most controversial. People who take the assessment get hung up on the word "best" because they think that means only having one friend instead of several. Gallup changed the word "best," as they found it might indicate leaving others out. When they attempted to change it to "close" or "good," it lost its effectiveness. Thus, "best" was reinstated and supports effective teamwork and engagement.

Gallup also discovered having a best friend at work meant that employees were:

1. 43 percent more likely to report having received praise in the last week.

2. 37 percent more likely to report that someone at work encourages their development.

3. 35 percent more likely to report coworker commitment to quality.

4. 27 percent more likely to report that the mission of their company makes them feel that their job is important.

Organizations must have managers involved to support these connections that effect both the individual's well-being and the company's bottom line. They can do this by promoting collaboration, being seen in the social activities of the company, and finding ways for the employees to get to know each other.

Helping others to connect allows them the opportunity to do what they do best every day. I invite you to contact me for suggestions on how to integrate deeper connections in your organization.

|································|

Analyze the benefits of the friendship
factor in your organization.

10. "YOU'VE GOT MAIL"

*"You can make more friends in two months by becoming more
interested in other people than you can in two years
by trying to get people interested in you."*

—Dale Carnegie, American writer, interpersonal skills

I have many nostalgic memories from the 1989 American romantic comedy, *When Harry Met Sally* and the famous words, "You've got mail." Connectivity was just beginning to become powerful. How quickly things change!

In a business, emails are sent to outside customers and inside employees. How are your emails being delivered and received? Emails are meant to create an opportunity, make an appointment, or confirm a meeting. Your emails can brand you and create your reputation.

Thus, consider what might create a better response to your inside and outside customers. Creativity! Write an email that is creative and leads the reader to want to read it and respond. Getting to know your prospect and your inside customer is the key to beginning.

CONNECTION YOU!

1. Do your research! Take time to research your customers on Facebook, YouTube, LinkedIn, Twitter, and Instagram to get all the information you can possibly obtain to "know" your potential internal/external customer. Find a way to engage them based on your research.

2. Cut it down! People are multitasking; get their attention in a few words. Most word processing programs will check the word count. The shorter, the better.

3. What is your value to the recipient? All emails should convey this.

4. What is your subject line? One word might be impactful. I often use my name so they will know it is not just junk mail: "From Sheila Stabile."

5. Is it a follow-up email? Keep your message short with the critical information in a pdf document.

6. Is it a follow up through email? Try to build personal connection with customers by asking to meet for coffee or phone call. Do you have a photo of the two of you to attach? Can you mention anything in common like a hobby, an event, or family?

Your emails can brand you and can be a vehicle for deeper connection.

|································|

Consider every business email you write,
"What is the value for my recipient?"

11. REMOTE WORKER CONNECTION

Don't be afraid to go out on a limb. That's where the fruit is.
—H. Jackson Browne, author, *Life's Little Instruction Book*

More companies are adding the ability for their employees to work remotely in order to be competitive and recruit the best talent. Companies are implementing a variety of ways to connect to their remote workers to create a culture of appreciation and ensure that it is beneficial for both the company and employee.

With the advances in technology, such as file sharing, instant messaging, and videoconferences, it has become much easier to work remotely. It can cut costs on office space and office interruptions. However, you often miss the ability to for the face-to-face interaction or the casual chance conversations around the water fountain.

In his book *Remote: Office Not Required*, Jason Fried offers tips for connecting remotely:

- Try to make sure that employees on different zones have about four hours of overlap in working hours.
- Create a "virtual water cooler" chat forum for fun and social interaction.
- Share progress with each other to fuel that sense of achievement and momentum.
- Consider a hybrid strategy, with some working in the office and some at home.

It could also be valuable to create scheduled interaction times to simply chat and express your appreciation. Employees will feel more connected by being asked how life is going or their weekend activities.

To make it a win-win working solution, companies must continue to explore ways to create a culture of connection for remote workers to enable a balanced approach. Putting systems in place so that the employees work the same way, whatever their location, helps keep the culture consistent. The investment of continuing to enhance the connection will pay off for the company and tenure of the employee.

|·······························|

Take the time to communicate with employees in a different physical location.

12. SPONTANEOUS COMBUSTION

Success isn't a result of spontaneous combustion.
You must set yourself on fire.

—Arnold H. Glasow, famous businessman

In science, spontaneous combustion is a process by which a collection of materials, such as oily rags, catches fire without the application of heat from outside. The oxidation of substances in the materials starts the fire.

Can humans spontaneously burst into conversation to create connection? I believe they can. Recently during a meeting in a downtown Washington, DC office building, the fire alarm caused our workshop attendees to evacuate. As we were all standing on the sidewalk outside waiting for the meeting to resume, I walked around and found only one person who was not looking down on their phone and with whom I could begin to start a conversation freely. I approached her and began a dialogue about the fire alarm. We then shared our names, reasons we were attending the workshop, and our entrepreneurial interests. I learned about new websites where I could go for information related to a project I had in the near future. We exchanged business cards and later shared emails with information that helped each other with various interests related to our goals.

To combust, a human body needs two things: intensely high heat and a flammable substance. To connect, we need two or more of us to be present to start a conversation and ignite chemistry that creates a bond on some level. Had this been a real fire and not just an alarm, we all most likely would have been taking care and protecting each other from harm. Why wait until it is an emergency to make a connection? In situations like this, where the fire alarm goes off and we have unexpected time, we can use the opportunity to be spontaneous, to connect, and perhaps kindle a friendship or business opportunity.

Learning to be more mindful in unexpected situations—like a fire, a break, or a chance meeting—may create possible business opportunities.

Here are good tinder materials to keep the connection burning:

1. Why are you here?
2. How did you hear about this workshop?

12. SPONTANEOUS COMBUSTION

3.   Have you ever had a fire drill in a workshop before?

If you don't want the fire to go out with a new connection, keep finding good tinder. You can learn to be spontaneous.

|································|

Inject spontaneity into unexpected opportunities to create connection.

13. CREATING EMOTIONAL TIES

Try to be a rainbow in someone's cloud.
—Maya Angelou, American memoirist

In customer service, there is a saying: "Aim for your customers' hearts and not just their heads."

The Gallup organization produced an article entitled "Customer Service Doesn't Count." In the article, it stated, "If you do not make an emotional connection with customers, then satisfaction is worthless." For true connection, it is important to engage customers or your audience at an emotional level. Do something they will remember—be different!

During my sales career, my goal was to give a personal touch to my customers whenever possible. I wanted them to know that I appreciated them and to relay my sincerity to them. One effort that was often well received was when I dropped off a box of fortune cookies. I would put a little note on the box and write, "I am fortunate to have you as a customer."

Sometimes it would be the factory fortunes cookies or I would personalize the fortunes within the cookies. Nonetheless, it was novel to my customers and created a connection we could further engage. From the reactions I received, it was obvious no other sales representative had done this.

In a recent Disney blog, I read the story of "The Purple Balloon." A family brought their two children to Disney, one being autistic who was sometimes easily overwhelmed. Upon one visit, the young son noticed something he really wanted, a clear balloon with a smaller purple Mickey balloon inside. The parents promised that if he was good, he would receive it at the end of the night.

After a day of rides and excitement, it was time to find the purple balloon. There were none in sight. A cast member saw that the mother was clearly in distress and beckoned a fellow cast member who reappeared a few minutes later with a purple balloon. The emotion that filled *THAT* family, *THAT* day with *THAT* balloon was priceless.

Connecting with prospects, customers, and employees at an emotional level can make your business a happy and memorable place, too.

What is your purple balloon? What is your fortune cookie?

|·····························|

*Engage customers on an emotional level
for a special connection.*

14. WIN SALES—
BOOST SINCERITY

Ask yourself a question: is my attitude worth catching?

—Zig Ziglar, motivational speaker

How often have you purchased something or made a transaction and you say, *"Have a nice day?"* Is it automatic for you? Do you sincerely mean it or perhaps you don't know what else to say or could it be automatic response?

Offering a sincere response can stimulate new and authentic connections. Consider the activities where you may communicate. On a recent trip, I paid close attention as I boarded the plane, ordered my food, did shopping, stopped at the bank, and rode in the taxi. Interactions give the opportunity to make a difference and be remembered.

As you become more aware of all your interactions, you can be more intentional about your message. If you do repeat business, people will remember you and they will want to do business because you stand out, offer sincerity, creativity, and perhaps want a "piece" of not only what you are "selling," but a portion of you! Your vulnerability and authenticity speak volumes.

This translates to sales. I love doing business with companies that show sincerity, remember me, make eye contact. After the sale, shaking my hand firmly, bringing the bag to the other side of the counter, and sending a thank-you for my purchase.

Think about what you can do differently: offer a kind word, notice something they are wearing, comment on something in the environment, or perhaps even share a light joke or jingle.

This makes me remember Southwest Airlines and how they make the passengers laugh while going through their boarding routine. Isn't it great how they create smiles?

We often can be robotic in our approach, yet with some creativity and sincerity we can stand out, be remembered, and win business or make a connection that improves our lives. Consider your message, exhibit your differentiation, and show your value for deeper connection.

|································|

Craft a sincere and creative message through words and actions.

15. WALKING MEETINGS

Walking is good for solving problems—it's like the feet are little psychiatrists.

—Pepper Giardino, author

"Walk and talk" is a new trend. Every day, I look for ways to maximize walking. I often wake up early and take a long walk, either doing meditation or listening to a book on Audible. When I am at home taking calls, I walk around my home. I like to work and talk on my feet and feel more energy as well. I park in spaces farther from my destination. Returning business phone calls on my walks allows a fresh air perspective.

A walking meeting is a meeting that takes place during a walk instead of across a desk or table. The average worker sits for eight to ten hours a day. Trading walking meetings for sitting meetings have had great success.

Research has found that walking increases creative thinking.

It can lead to better connection and employee engagement. Steve Jobs and Mark Zuckerberg have also endorsed walking meetings to improve worker energy and engagement. Business editor Nilofer Merchant in her TED Talk, "Got a meeting? Take a Walk" suggests that walking might have a big impact on your health, as we sleep almost as much as we sit.

Some meetings still require paper and pencils and whiteboards. One needs to plan ahead for the weather and the right clothing. Whenever you can incorporate walking meetings, here are some benefits to consider:

- Side-by-side meetings are good for one-on-ones
- Nature will often let silence promote thoughtfulness
- Create personal connections
- Boost of energy
- Hierarchical boundaries can lessen
- Inspiration

If walking creates better connection, reduced risk of dementia, breast and colon cancer, and heart disease, it's pretty convincing to incorporate it in business and life.

|······························|

*Boost connection, creativity, and health
by incorporating walking meetings.*

REFLECTIONS ON CONNECTING AT WORK

1. Based on reading the section "Connection at Work," what are two things you could begin implementing to enhance connection within your organization?

_____

_____

_____

_____

_____

_____

_____

_____

2. Think about a connection that has been positive for your organization. List reasons why and consider how you may apply it to other opportunities.

_____

_____

_____

_____

_____

_____

_____

_____

3. What is one thing you can implement for the well-being of your organization or customers?

_____

_____

_____

_____

_____

_____

_____

_____

4. Research has shown that loneliness and social isolation are on the rise. What are ways you could create awareness within your organization to be inclusive?

_____

_____

_____

_____

_____

_____

_____

5. Technology addiction is on the rise. What are ways you could implement awareness techniques to enhance human interaction and connection versus technology?

_____

_____

_____

_____

_____

_____

_____

6. Based upon the recommendations in this book, what training programs, assessments, and books can you implement for better connection?

_____

_____

_____

_____

_____

_____

_____

_____

CONNECTING AT
WORK ACTION LIST

Make time to allow for deeper employee relationships— Structure activities that will increase employee socialization. Provide half-day workshops or extended lunches that encourage your employees to interact and get the chance to know each other better.

Add uniqueness and pizzazz for your customers— Explore ways that make you stand out in appreciating your customers in a unique fashion. Think of gifts, traditions, seminars, letters. Focus on creating that unique connection that will deepen and maintain connection with them.

Encourage reading for education and connection— This can be done as a book group or in small groups. Find ways to share what you have learned. Post the book titles and allow your employees to add their comments.

Give talent assessments—Get to know your team's strengths. Consider Gallup's CliftonStrengths assessment or another on the market. Hire a coach to help you administer and share the results that will reveal strengths and growth opportunities to collaborate.

Remember your remote workers—Don't let out of sight be out of mind. Call them, conference them in, post their faces, schedule regular connection with other on-site employees. Include them in team activities.

Write hand-written notes—These are great for managers to provide touchpoints to your organization. This improves connection, appreciation, and the bottom line.

PART 2
CONNECTION IN LIFE

INTRODUCTION

Connections give purpose and meaning to our lives.

— Brené Brown

We were born to connect! It is one of our fundamental human needs. Research has shown that people who are the happiest and healthiest are those who have strong connections with friends, family, and community. Connection is essential to our well-being and finding people to connect with makes us feel good. Social connection allows us to have better health, a longer life, and increased happiness.

Research has shown that social isolation and loneliness are on the rise. This will most likely only grow with the increase of social media and the increase in remote workers in the workforce. The dangers of isolation and loneliness are frightening, including addiction, depression, and suicide.

Although technology has improved our lives in some ways, it has caused us to disconnect. The urges to constantly check social media are higher than ever, supporting our need to connect, as we have cultural pressures to be constantly updated on the latest messages and news. We are decreasing eye-to-eye contact and the ability to read body language that allows us to have deeper connections.

Answer these questions honestly:

- Have you texted someone instead of meeting them?

- Have you ever texted an important person in your life instead of meeting them?

- Have you ever ignored someone around you because you were texting?

This is the world today. We are losing human connection. When we focus on connecting in life, we need to make relationships count. Technology will always be there for us; people will not.

Maurice Sendak, in *The Wild Things*, wrote, "Let the Royal Rumpus Start!" We can increase our connection personally while enhancing the lives of our family and friends. Yet, the rumpus really begins when we go beyond our immediate circle and infect the lives in our community. People out there need us. We need them. A few moments of your time could make the difference in someone's day or life.

May these stories begin the inspiration within you to increase connection.

16. DANGER: SELFIE STICKS

*The best thing about a picture is that it never changes,
even when the people in it do.*

—Andy Warhol, American artist

During a recent visit to the Grand Canyon with my son, I was shocked to observe how many people had selfie sticks. It was a bit scary to watch them angling them so close to the edge of the boulders. Not only was it a bit frightening, the sticks were taking up room so that others could not move freely and causing traffic jams in areas.

We took the plunge to ask other visitors to take our photos. Most smiled and also asked for reciprocation of a photo. We talked with people from Japan, Australia, and Michigan. We learned about lodging and other tourist sites in the Grand Canyon area. If we had used selfie sticks, we would not have had this exchange or connection to the area.

The New York Times recently published an article about

museum officials across the country that have banned selfie sticks, as they were concerned about safety and art.

The Hirschhorn Museum and Sculpture Garden in Washington prohibited the sticks this month, and the Museum of Fine Arts in Houston plans to impose a ban. In New York, the Metropolitan Museum of Art, which has been studying the matter for some time, has just decided that it, too, will forbid selfie sticks. (New signs will be posted soon.)

Not only can selfie sticks be dangerous, people who use them and snapping their own photos are not aware of their relationship to the people around them.

Pizza Hut recently highlighted the dangers and consequences of selfie sticks on a video. You can watch it at https://www.youtube.com/watch?v=4cI3gycfcRw.

There are many advantages to reaching out to another person to take a picture. You most likely will get a better picture; you give an opportunity to connect to another person and might help that person too afraid to ask. Putting down the selfie stick and asking someone to take our photo allows people to authentically experience and interact with others, making a new connection that can benefit ourselves.

⊢·····························⊣

Take the opportunity to connect with others by asking them to take your photo.

17. INTERGENERATIONAL CONNECTIONS

Tell me and I'll forget. Show me and I may remember.
Involve me and I learn.

—Benjamin Franklin, Founding Father of the United States

Intergenerational friendships offer rich rewards. They offer opposing perspectives and a lens through which you can look at different experiences. Both parties can benefit from this special kind of engagement.

Before you can reap the rewards of intergenerational friendships, you must cultivate them.

Take, for example, some thoughts of my friend, Kathy, who recently was asked by her family to give a eulogy for her older friend Mary's funeral. Mary was a neighbor of Kathy's and their introduction took place when Kathy was struggling to start a lawnmower. Mary came over from next door to assist and announced, "There's no spark in the spark plug."

In the eulogy, Kathy shared, "Giving was easy for Mary. Sharing her time, talents, and wisdom came naturally. Life struggles made her strong, fiercely independent, and self-sufficient.

"Receiving help was NOT easy for Mary. In her later years, there were times when she realized that even she had limits. She reluctantly accepted help but wasn't satisfied unless she could find some way of paying back. If you would not take money or a meal, she figured out you would never turn down a gift of one of her German chocolate cakes or brownies." Kathy continued her eulogy, "I was sad we decided to move in 2002, as we were used to seeing Mary every day and she was widowed. Our solution was a 6:45 a.m. phone date. These calls brought us closer and I learned a lot of wisdom that she had to share. This included learning about her internal alarm clock of between four and five each morning and the routines that were important to her. Daily she would make a healthy breakfast, read her scriptures, do her laundry, and exercise. Should we all be so disciplined with our daily lives! To know Mary was to know goodness. My life is richer because of her and now that she is gone, so is a little piece of my heart."

There is a beautiful reciprocity with intergenerational connections. Theresa Carey, a screenwriter, once wrote, "My younger friends connect me to where I've been, and my older friends connect me to where I am going."

2. INTERGENERATIONAL CONNECTIONS

As Kathy and Mary took the time to cultivate their intergenerational friendship, they both reaped the rewards and deepened their connection. They are both winners and both enriched their lives.

|································|

*Cultivate intergenerational connections
to thrive and grow.*

18. RECONNECTING TO YOUR UNIVERSITY

Re-visioning begins with a look back to remember and reconnecting with one's core identity and ongoing story.

—Dr. John C. Bowling, ONU president

College is where we spend several years of our life. Taking an opportunity to visit your alma mater might produce some nostalgia or perhaps allow you to become reengaged both to the progress of the university and alumni.

Keeping alumni engaged is both a benefit to the institution and the alumni. The university can benefit from the experiences of the graduates, their financial support, and encouraging their graduates to be ambassadors to their personal and professional networks.

I recently attended a President's Gathering as an alumnus of Olivet Nazarene University. I attended primarily because of the university's efforts in keeping me engaged. The gathering was small enough to be able to network with many people and speak one-on-one with the guest speakers and college personnel. Reacquainting myself allowed me to know more about the incredible work the university continues to achieve, including increased enrollment and programs. I also benefitted by reconnecting with graduates and meeting new individuals connected to the university by marriage or otherwise, which gave me new insight into both personal and business ideas.

Here are some ideas to connect and reconnect to your university:

1. Join your university's alumni group. This may be direct through your school or through LinkedIn (it may be in a group directory).

2. Investigate a magazine or online alumni newsletter.

3. Seek opportunities to become involve with your university students. This is both a volunteer opportunity and creates new connections for you.

4. Engage in social media sites that allow alumni to connect, reminisce, and share.

5. Participate in networking events that might be in your area sponsored by the university.

6. Attend a special event at your university, such as a lecture, cultural, or sports event.

7. Communicate with development officers at your university and share you are interested in becoming reacquainted.

3. RECONNECTING TO YOUR UNIVERSITY

ONE contact, ONE inspiration could make a difference in your life or the life of someone else. There is much potential in dusting off our old rolodex.

Get curious, be open, and connect to your university! I was apprehensive after many years to reengage; however, it was truly a return on my university investment both from a heart and business encounter. Change is good; it can rekindle connection.

|································|

Reconnect to your university
for unexpected insights.

19. SPOOKTACULAR CONNECTIONS

Never, ever underestimate the importance of having fun.

—Randy Pausch, professor of human-computer interaction

Halloween is one of the highest-grossing commercial holidays and Party City accounts 25 percent of its business to this spooky day. Halloween is good for business and it is also a day to connect with others in a cheerful and memorable way.

There are many social and psychological benefits of dressing up:

- Enjoy office and neighborhood parties
- Wear without being judged
- Create imaginative play
- Relive your childhood
- Relieve stress
- Create simple, inexpensive enjoyment

- Allow fun conversation starters

Going to parties, socializing, and creating a costume allows you to make new friends and have fun with longtime friends and neighbors. Another indicator is the connection that Halloween brings. It provides an easier way to connect with others in a fun way while creating traditions and memories. The pet industry reports that there is an increase in people also dressing their pets on Halloween to add to the rituals.

Halloween is an escape from our busy, stressful lives. What a joy to watch people smiling and having fun. What other day of the year can you experience Superman and Mary Poppins driving cars? Other activities to enjoy are watching people striving to win costume contests on TV shows. In my neighborhood, a party was planned every year for the adults and children, bringing neighbors young and old together as a community and created long-lasting memories.

There is power in the costume. There is power in being silly and imaginative. Everything is easier when you feel connected to other people and especially when we add humor and laughter. Start planning now for next Halloween.

|⋅⋅⋅⋅⋅⋅⋅⋅⋅⋅⋅⋅⋅⋅⋅⋅⋅⋅⋅⋅⋅⋅⋅⋅⋅⋅⋅⋅⋅⋅|

Dress up on Halloween and spread joy
from person to person.

20. JUST FOR THE HEALTH OF IT

Every time you communicate, you have an opportunity to influence people's lives for the better.

—Victoria Labalme, performance artist and coach

When you are in your daily routine and least suspect it, yet aware of your surroundings, you just might meet someone noteworthy. This happened to me, in all places, at the Target store when I stopped to pick up a few items for my home. I was in the check-out line organizing my purchases, when I looked behind me and glanced at what seemed to be a recognizable face. I took a second look, tried a chance at conversation and inquired, "Has anyone ever told you that you look like the famous Dr. Weil?" He replied, "I **am** Dr. Weil." Dr. Andrew Weil is a celebrity doctor who is a physician, author, spokesperson, and guru of holistic health. He has written many books, blogs, and appeared on many talk shows sharing his health tips. Generally, I usually think it is polite to give famous people their space; however, I was so excited of this chance meeting that I asked the Target employee to take our picture. In good stead, he agreed.

The photo opportunity allowed me a few minutes of conversation, and I learned he was in town for the grand opening of his new restaurant, True Food Kitchen, which was across the street. True Food features dishes that closely adhere to Dr. Weil's anti-inflammatory diet.

The timing of people coming into our lives may be coincidence; however, you can turn it into the opportunity for a meaningful connection. Meeting Dr. Weil did not bring me more money in my career. However, it provided me personal happiness to meet him, allowed me to post on my Facebook page, creating one of the "most liked" entries to date, which created connection and inspiration with my followers. This also gave Dr. Weil free publicity about his new restaurant. It was a win-win encounter.

I took the suggestion of my new connection's advice and went across the street to give True Kitchen a try. Naturally, I had to share my iPhone photo from Target with some of the staff and customers I was sitting close to and embellished the story of meeting Dr. Weil. I made a few additional connections. Just for the health of it, I ordered the Tuscan Kale Salad. It was delicious.

|································|

Pay attention for the opportunity of chance meetings to increase connections.

21. KINDNESS THE GATSBY WAY

A little party never killed nobody.

—F. Scott Fitzgerald, author, *The Great Gatsby*

Our connections can be strengthened when we are kind to people. Kindness is contagious and a morale booster in clubs, work, or home settings. It provides both the recipient and the givers a warm and fuzzy feeling. Our society flourishes when people look out for one another. Kindness can be fun. Kindness adds connectedness.

Recently I was cochair of a Holiday Ball with the theme "Gatsby." The participants came adorned dressed in the 1920's clothing resembling just what you saw in the original Gatsby movie, with pearls, headpieces, cigarette holders, sequins, and lace. There were large feather table arrangements and Radio King Orchestra provided a ten-piece band sharing music from the era. All the ingredients for this party spelled f-u-n.

One member from our club, a former party planner, was sadly unable to attend due to recent chemotherapy treatments for a Stage IV cancer. A group of members from the club decided to take the Gatsby party to her on another afternoon. We adorned ourselves with some of our Gatsby attire, including the headbands and pearls used at the original party, while securing one of the feather arrangements we used as the day's centerpiece. We recreated the night, organized food and fun, then caravanned to her home.

What we recreated positively impacted our friend, who was healing as well as each of us who participated. When we become aware of how much influence we have by sharing kindness, we improve ourselves and elevate the lives of others.

Do not underestimate the healing power of a shared meal, kindness, laughter, and just plain fun that can share in recovering health. We are made for love and compassion. One of the group participants suggested that perhaps we develop a home visit like this to others in the future who might have a similar situation. This type of connection can reach one at the personal level while expanding to group connection.

When we look out for one another, we flourish. Making concerted efforts to stay connected and offering kindness is contagious and can reach many lives. Add a little creativity to the kindness for everyone's benefit that will long be remembered.

|································|

Strengthen your connection through kindness and add a dash of party for the memory.

22. LISTEN UP!

*We have two ears and one tongue so that we
would listen more and talk less.*

—Diogenes, Greek philosopher

Listening skills are vital to your success in life and impact a company's interaction with customers and their businesses. Listening can make us better leaders, better conversationalists, and often make you the most-liked person in the room.

Listening is different than hearing. It requires you to shut out distractions and focus on the other person. Good eye contact is essential in listening, as that is where the real connection occurs, and makes the other person feel important.

Harvey Mackay is the author of *The New York Times* number-one bestsellers *Swim with the Sharks Without Being Eaten Alive* and *Beware the Naked Man Who Offers You His Shirt*. On a recent webcast, he was describing that one of the top success tips he offers is listening to others. He advised listeners to not try to top someone's story and don't finish someone else's story. In the book *Blink*, by Malcom Gladwell, he states that impressions are made in a blink of an eye. It could be during that few seconds of inattentiveness that we lose someone.

The International Listening Association (ILA) was formed in 1979 and has since grown into an international community working in more than nineteen countries. They are involved in listening in education, business, healthcare, hospitality, spirituality, music, and many other fields. The International Listening Association serves as a space for networking, resources, and community. Statistics from the ILA website includes:

- Most listeners only recall 50 percent of what they have heard immediately after hearing someone say it.
- People spend 45 percent of their waking time listening.
- Most people only remember about 20 percent of what they hear over time.
- Eighty-five percent of our learning is derived from listening.
- Listening is an important component in how people judge communicative competence in the workplace.

Listening is critical to academic, personal, and business

success. Fortunately, listening is a skill people can learn. Body language expert Jan Hargrove shares the four tenets of listening:

- Eye contact (fully engage)
- Presence (try to keep mind from shifting)
- Nonverbal feedback (try to keep your mind from shifting)
- Lean in (promotes better nonverbal connection)

Listening is a skill and will always be a lifelong goal to perfect. Some of my best relationships were established by being open to have a conversation.

Sometimes the best answer you can give others is a pair of ears.

|································|

Foster good listening skills to build a successful business and brand positioned to thrive.

23. SOCIAL ISOLATION AND LONELINESS

We all need each other.
—Leo Buscaglia, aka "Dr. Love"

Social isolation is a growing epidemic and one that has severe physical and emotional consequences. According to the AARP Foundation, one in five Americans sixty-five and older are socially isolated. New research suggests that social isolation and separating ourselves from others is detrimental to our well-being. People with less social connection have more health problems, including disrupted sleep patterns and shorter life spans. Social isolation begins when people withdraw and become disconnected with family and friends.

Some of the most common effects of not feeling a connection to others include feeling lonely frequently, depression, being sick more often, and generally decreased energy. Dr. John Cacioppo, a psychology professor at the

University of Chicago, has tested different ways to treat loneliness. He shares that one of the most effective ways is to help people look deeper in how they interact with others and interpret social cues. He is collaborating with the United States military to study how social cognition training can help soldiers feel less isolated when they return home.

Being cognizant of ourselves and others is a beginning to assist with this growing epidemic. A program started at the Palo Alto Medical Foundation called linkages.org is a cross-generational service exchange with the philosophy that everyone has something to offer. Individuals post online something they want help with, such as rides or music lessons, then others volunteer time and skills to answer those requests.

Research has demonstrated it is clear that human connection foster well-being. Analyzing our personal relationships and our communities to find where we may make a difference to decrease others' loneliness could be a beginning of helping someone else and creating greater connection for ourselves.

Sharing our experiences makes life richer. Humans are born to be connected. It is essential to find ways to reach out to others and help them connect. Rick Bateman, in his blog, "Social Wellness," states "It's not the chicken soup that makes you better; it's the person who brings you the chicken soup."

|································|

Maintain bonds and create new ones
to decrease social isolation.

24. SOLE TO SOUL

The right shoes can change your life.

—Cinderella

Shoes have always fascinated me. Often shoes are a first impression we give someone or notice on others. They carry nonverbal communication and cues that can be great conversation starters. Shoes can create connection in your life and lead to developing relationships.

You can learn a lot about strangers by checking out their footwear. At a Nordstrom's shoe department, while trying on multiple pairs of shoes, I began a conversation about shoes with another customer, Katherine. She made a great first impression with her choice of style. Our initial conversations led us to great dialogue about shoes including price, color, apparel, and even movies.

That conversation was a first step that grew into a valuable friendship and business relationship several years later and remains today. From that shoe encounter grew a lunch date at a later time. We continued to build on our friendship both socially and in business. We have served as sources of support for each other in business and life. Additionally, other business and social introductions were made. Our connection grew from sole to soul.

As the researchers explained in the *Journal of Research in Personality,* "Shoes serve a practical purpose, and also serve as nonverbal cues with symbolic messages. People tend to pay attention to the shoes they and others wear." Many people make shoe contact before eye contact.

Connections can be made with shoe conversations and you can meet interesting people, as well as a friend for life like me!

Here are some shoe conversation starters:

- "Wow, those shoes look great on you!"
- "Where did you find a pair of shoes like that?"
- "You have great taste in shoes."
- "What is the name of your podiatrist?"
  (Then you smile.)

Perhaps Cinderella might have been on to something when she said, "The right shoes can change your life."

|································|

Pay attention to shoes; they carry symbolic messages that can lead to valuable first impressions and connections.

25. TECHNOLOGY ADDICTION AND CONNECTION

The human spirit must prevail over technology.

—Albert Einstein, Theoretical physicist

The term "Technology Addiction" has been added to the Diagnostic and Statistical Manual of Mental Disorders. The term Technology Addiction is an umbrella term for online and smartphone overuse.

The International Journal of Neuropsychiatric Medicine states that one in eight Americans suffers from problematic Internet use. This addiction can bring on chemical changes in the brain similar to those caused by substance abuse. According to the Pew Internet Project, 58 percent of adults and 37 percent of teens have smartphones, which is a big contributor to technology addiction.

Hilarie Cash, Ph.D., cofounder of the Internet Addiction Recovery Program, stated symptoms can include:

- Compulsive checking of text messages

- Frequent "selfies" on Facebook
- A feeling of euphoria while on the web
- Social withdrawal
- Feelings of restlessness when unable to go online

This behavior is widespread and concerning about the way we connect or do not connect. It has caused changes in meetings, theatre, dinners, families, and activities. I have been in several social situations where I have observed the body was present but the mind was not. People take pictures and interrupt the flow of connection and conversation.

The Enough is Enough (EIE) (https://enough.org/) mission is to make the Internet safer for children and families. They are dedicated to promoting child dignity in the digital world by raising public awareness about the harms of Internet pornography, sexual predators, cyberbullying, and other dangers.

The evidence is there for us to be conscious of our own behavior and that of our loved ones. Being addicted to technology can be associated to addiction to alcohol or other drugs or pornography, with many of the same effects of brain development. Being conscious of our technology and the way we connect, as well as the effect on others, is worth pondering. The power of the Internet is literally in the palm of our hands.

|······························|

Consider how technology connection may affect you "being present."

26. THE OPPOSITE OF ADDICTION IS CONNECTION

*In the end we won't be measured by our bank account
but by the difference we made in people's lives.*

—Jon Gordon, author

Addiction has been defined many ways and experts have a multitude of philosophies on how one might develop an addiction. An interesting perspective on addiction has surfaced from Johann Harri, author of *Chasing the Scream* and his TED Talk, *Everything you Know About Addiction Is Wrong.* "The opposite of addiction is not sobriety. The opposite of addiction is connection." His theory is the cause of addiction to both drugs or your mobile device is a lack of connection.

Many scientists, including Dr. Peter Cohen and Dr. Gabor Maté, support this finding. Their studies show the role of trauma and emptiness with individuals numbing themselves with substances to get rid of their pain. They reference the lack of relationship and connection in explaining what drives people to become addicted to drugs or something else.

"Human beings have a natural and innate need to bond. And when we're happy and healthy, we'll bond and connect with each other," Hari explained. "But if you can't do that—because you're traumatized or isolated or beaten down by life—you will bond with something that will give you some sense of relief. Now that might be gambling, that might be pornography, that might be cocaine, that might be cannabis, but you will bond and connect with something because that's our nature, that's what we want as human beings."

The addiction treatment community supports this finding. Going through AA (Alcoholics Anonymous) requires going through a 12-step recovery program. It involves connecting to other people in a safe and supportive environment.

In Hari's TED Talk, he shares how Portugal decriminalized drugs and took a different approach. Instead of spending money on incarceration, it channeled its efforts into helping those with addictions connect with society with trial jobs and social support. Their goal was to reintegrate them into communities, helping them to learn to trust and connect once again. Reports show the program has been effective and the addicts have felt more valued.

These findings support that human beings crave connection. Many of us know a person close or a loved one with an addiction, thus this should cause us pause. Striving to maintain unconditional love until they are able to have the self-love and embrace their value and connection to the world can be powerful. We can all seek to be part on one's supportive network. We are all in this together.

|································|

Consider if there is a support network in which you could make a difference.

27. VOLUNTEERISM

Service to others is the rent you pay for your room here on earth.

—Muhammad Ali, professional boxer

Volunteering increases your connections, *widens* your world to others, may help with career changes, and offers the opportunity to explore new industries often without risk. It can also bring great health benefits including stress reduction, reduced risks of depression, and boost self-confidence. It gets you moving, staying physically and mentally active. You simply can become more interesting by volunteering!

Henry McKay, in his book *Swim With the Sharks,* shared that his father gave him some of the best advice he had ever received. His father told him that if he focused on others, he would never have trouble finding opportunities. He shares that volunteering has made his life better and he believes it has made him a better salesperson, speaker, and leader.

A study from Carnegie Mellon University showed that volunteering regularly reduced blood pressure. When researchers at the London School of Economics examined the relationship between volunteering and happiness, they found out that the more people volunteered, the happier they were *(Small Changes, Big Rewards)*.

Volunteering for me has increased my leadership skills, speaking opportunities, grew my network, utilized my skills for the betterment of others, and expanded my knowledge of the geographical area. When you speak and volunteer you may not know people, but people get to know you.

Presenting your best in your volunteer position is also a good indication of how you represent yourself professionally. Judy Robinette, author of *How to Be a Power Connector*, shares: "When you deliver first-class work as a volunteer, people will assume you deliver the same high-quality work in your professional life."

Start volunteering to make friends, improve your mental and physical health, and develop new skills along the way, You can change your life and the lives of others when you do.

|································|

Volunteer to improve your health, happiness, and become more interesting.

28. WHAT'S IN A NAME?

What's in a name? That which we call a rose by any other name would smell as sweet.

—William Shakespeare, author, *Romeo and Juliet*

The power of a name and its value has long been used in prose and poetry. Universally everyone recognizes himself or herself by name. A name can influence everything from school activities, who you meet, who you remember, and perhaps even marry!

Names can make positive and negative impressions. One thing is for sure, everyone loves to be acknowledged by name and it is a great way to connect. It is even better if you attach a meaning to it.

In some of the workshops I facilitate, I use an icebreaker activity in which I have everyone introduce themselves to the group. Each person tells the group a story about their name. Participants sometimes share how they were named, who named them, and why and if their name had a positive or negative influence in their life. It's a great way for people to remember each other and have instant connection.

I met a friendly couple at a recent gathering. Their names were Nancy and Merle Bright. Nancy signed her name NanSEA, as she lived by the water and had a boat named after her. I suggested to both of them it must be great to have a last name of always being "Bright." Merle quickly responded that his friends often call him Hardly. It will be easy to remember NanSEA and Hardly Bright!

Do you notice when you call someone's name that they automatically look at you? The next time you are challenged to make conversation or have a special reason why you want to remember someone or to be remembered, ignite a name conversation. It can be fascinating what you may learn for a lifelong connection.

|································|

Use a person's name to be ensured of being remembered.

29. WHO IS
YVETTE VICKERS?

*People crave comfort, people crave connection,
people crave community.*

—Marianne Williamson, spiritual teacher

Yvette Vickers is a B-movie star, best known for her role in
Attack of the 50-Foot Woman.

The Los Angeles coroner's office reported that she lay dead
for the better part of a year before a neighbor noticed
cobwebs and yellowed letters in her mailbox. She was found
mummified, upstairs with her computer still running.

Although she had 16,057 Facebook posts and 881 tweets,
she suffered from the growing amount of documented
loneliness. She had no children, no known social groups,
and no spiritual or religious attachment, and looked to the
computer for her connection.

She was found dead in her home by a concerned neighbor who
climbed through a broken window and many cobwebs to find

her. The neighbor stated, "She kept to herself, but still got cards from all over the world requesting her photo. All the neighbors are upset; no one should have to die like this. Nobody should be left alone like this." The phone of Yvette Vickers was still connected. Another neighbor reported, "We're all longtime neighbors here and we respect each other's privacy . . . perhaps too much."

Yvette Vickers received more attention in death than in life. Her connections were a web of strangers, which caused her to be lonelier.

Loneliness is on the rise and an increasing problem in the United States.

Extreme loneliness can increase an older person's chances of premature death by 14 percent and increases the risk of cognitive decline, elevated blood pressure and other health concerns. According to psychologist John Cacioppo, the leading professor of loneliness at the University of Chicago, his research identified three core items to healthy relationships: intimate connectedness, when someone affirms who you are; relational connectedness, which is face-to-face contacts; and collective connectedness that helps you feel you are part of a group.

Loneliness is a hidden killer. Humanizing our connections and reaching out and keeping in touch with friends, neighbors, and extended families is critical.

|································|

Consider what we can do as a community to reduce loneliness and increase connection.

30. HUMOR CONNECTS US

Laughter is the closest distance between two people.

—Victor Borge, American-Danish comedian

Laughter brings us together. It's often been said that laughter is the best medicine, as it has been noted to help improve blood pressure, reduce aggression, boost our immune system, and improve our mood and overall sense of well-being. When I heard laughter could tone my abs and burn calories, I was all in.

Laughing together strengthens our connections. Laughter is contagious and when we are around other people, we are able to laugh more. Thus the social element brings us health benefits as well. Laughing with others keeps our relationships healthy and fun and joyful.

I always like to keep a couple jokes in my memory bank to share when there is time to insert one in conversation. It changes the mood in conversations. One of my favorites is to ask, "What did the buffalo say to his son when he went off to college?" Of course, most say, "Not sure." The answer is "Bison." There is always a hesitation before the laughter.

You can create a couple stand-by jokes, too, even if you aren't "funny"! Regardless, if you don't consider yourself a humorous person, you can seek out those who make others laugh—many comedians (including myself) enjoy an audience!

Sharing sitcoms, games, and going to improv or comedy shows are also great ways to add humor to our relationships. Humor bonds. It sticks around, too.

Along with the physical benefits of laughter listed above, here are some social benefits that may encourage you to add humor to your life:

- Strengthens relationships
- Attracts others to us
- Enhances teamwork
- Helps defuse conflict
- Promotes group bonding
- Improves mood
- Adds joy and zest to life

So laugh, connect . . . knock, knock . . . Who's there?

|································|

Explore ways to add humor to your relationships for healthy connections.

REFLECTIONS ON CONNECTING IN LIFE

1. In this book, there are quotations and thoughts about building connections. What is one that resonates with you and why?

_____

_____

_____

_____

_____

_____

_____

_____

2. Give thought to what you might do or go to reach out to someone who is not in your immediate circle but who could be experiencing social isolation or loneliness. Write why you think this may be important to you and to the other person.

_____

_____

_____

_____

_____

_____

3. Plan a day that you will commit to putting your phone away for a period of time and communication with another person. It can be nonverbal; just be aware of the other person. This could be at a store, a drive-in lane, or at the dinner table. Write about your conscience effort. Evaluate your temptations, thoughts, and further goals around phone use.

_____

_____

_____

_____

_____

_____

4. Do you agree that technology interferes with you connecting?

_____

_____

_____

_____

_____

_____

5. What has been the most valuable message you have learned in *Connection You*?

_____

_____

_____

_____

_____

_____

6. Reread the story about those who have died alone and famous recluses. Consider connection or the lack of connection with these cases.

_____
_____
_____
_____
_____
_____

7. Do you agree that connection and well-being are related?

_____
_____
_____
_____
_____
_____

CONNECTING IN
LIFE ACTION LIST

Set technology limits for yourself—Consider a "detox vacation" from technology. Make your goal to decrease the checking of emails, phones, social media, and the temptation to post a photo immediately. It may need to be a partial detox. If you create a log of when you must connect, it will help you be accountable. Prepare for this by making a list of reading materials, exercise, and other curiosities that may be stored in your brain that you have wanted to do.

Talk to a stranger—Challenge yourself to be aware of others at a grocery store, mall, social activity, or other safe environment. Try giving someone a smile, a compliment, or ask a question. Create a short dialog about something that may be in the environment. This possibly could make someone's day, and in addition could also be beneficial to you by acquiring a new acquaintance, a new perspective on something. An act of connection can brighten a day and create a warm spark.

CONNECTION YOU!

Volunteer—Mother Teresa once said, "Help one person at a time, and always start with the person nearest you." Volunteering can help you discover your passions, often self-discovery of skills, and connection. People who do volunteer work have been known to have lower mortality rates and greater functional abilities. Volunteering can sometimes lead you to a new job and will help you be a better salesperson, leader, or whatever you are doing.

Never eat alone—The book *Never Eat Alone*, written by Keith Ferrazzi, has great insights into networking. He offers great advice in that eating meals with others and especially inviting new people to dine can provide opportunities to form greater relationships. This can apply to home and work. Keith suggests creative dinner topics to get to know others.

Exercise—Get moving, which can be productive for mental stress and also provide opportunities to meet others. Consider gyms or local walk/runs benefitting charities. Compare your steps on monitors together. Walking and bike riding are no-cost alternatives. Life is always better when shared, especially with exercise.

Take a class—This is a great opportunity to improve your well-being, think in new directions, become aware of new hobbies, and recognize and appreciate talents. This could open doors for new friends and new directions in your life. You learn and stay motivated. Who knows what this will connect to in your life.

Be mindful of someone who will not read this book—As mentioned, loneliness and isolation are at all-time highs. Be mindful of those who are not in your public eye. Ask questions of family members and friends who you have not seen in a while. There may be someone who needs you.

PART 3
CONNECTION WITH SELF

INTRODUCTION

Let us become the change we seek in the world.
—Mahatma Gandhi, Great Soul

Connecting with ourselves is more important than ever. The world is becoming more dependent on technology rather than human interaction. Loneliness and social isolation are at all-time highs. The joy of connecting with yourself increases happiness and peace.

Social media has changed the way we connect with each other. The desire and urge to connect to social media has replaced human interaction. The urge to check our social media or even the beep on our phone in steadily increasing, caused by our need to belong and connect. The need to "keep up" can lead us to feeling overwhelmed and create anxiety, a sign of our need to belong and connect.

Studies have shown that 61 percent of us admit to being addicted to the Internet and devices. One study suggested that the mere presence of one's smartphone reduces available cognitive capacity and impairs cognitive functioning. A silenced phone on a table can change the quality of a conversation—because people are reluctant to go deep and then be easily interrupted.

When we are so connected to our devices, we miss body language and decrease our empathy levels, causing a barrier to connection with others.

Loneliness and social interaction are on the rise. It is recognized of having mental, physical and emotional consequences. A study by AARP found that 35 percent of adults over forty-five were chronically lonely in contrast to ten years ago. Research in August 2017 from the American Psychological Association suggested that loneliness and social isolation could be a higher public health hazard than obesity. Both of these are expected to continue to rise in the future.

The joy of connecting with ourselves creates happiness and peace. Self-compassion is the genuine desire to contribute to our own and others' well-being.

31. ALL THE WORLD'S A STAGE

Life's like a movie; write your own ending.
Keep believing, keep pretending.

—Jim Henson, filmmaker

"All the world's a stage" is the phrase that begins a monologue from William Shakespeare's *As You Like It*, spoken by Jaques in Act II Scene VII. The speech compares the world to a stage and life to a play, and catalogues the seven stages of a man's life, sometimes referred to as the seven ages of man.

When I was growing up, one of my favorite pastimes was performing my own puppet shows. I would save the large cardboard boxes that my parents would have in the trash and would carve a big square in it to create an opening. My mom would sew curtains for me and I would pin them in the opening of the square to enable opening and closing just like the Broadway shows.

I would gather a few people, either my parents, one of my four siblings, or a neighbor to be my audience. Next, I would produce a "show" for them, either with my favorite hand puppets—Sherry Lewis's Hush Puppy, Lamb Chop, or Charlie Horse—or I would use my dolls or stuffed animals. At times, my show would duplicate something I had seen on television, a story from a book, or often I would "ad-lib." As I became more experienced, I added music and sounds from objects around the house like pans, spoons, and I even used the muffin tin as a drum. My shows would end with my audience's applause and a delightful, proud bow from me as I appeared now in front of the box. Later, as my confidence grew, I would carry the box around the neighborhood and ask people if they wanted puppet shows for a small fee.

My love for puppets and acting continued through high school, being awarded "honor thespian" upon graduation. I had no special training in puppet shows and they were not Oscar-nominated; however, as I look back on that time in my life, I think about the strong connection it afforded me. I connected with my imagination, which allowed me to connect deeper to the world around my audiences and me. I have since shared my puppet adventures with friends that have children and grandchildren and they have actually purchased the professional puppet show boxes for their kids. The puppet shows now have a legacy. Therapists sometimes use puppets as a form of therapy to get their patients to talk or express feelings. Others use puppets to engage people and delight in a more professional manner. Puppet shows can help connect the mind, body, and spirit. There is no age requirement for puppet shows and you don't have to have a box. It can happen at a sales meeting or the dinner table for interesting connection.

|································|

Consider a puppet show to engage others.

32. CONNECTING WITH CHILDHOOD MEMORIES

The most sophisticated people I know—
inside, they are children.

—Jim Henson, creator of The Muppets

Childhood, for most people, is the happiest times of our lives. We did not have jobs or responsibilities and there was plenty of time to learn and discover. We often lose our passions as we grow up.

When I was ready to change careers, I began to question myself about what my next steps should be. What excited me? Where could I make a difference? It was time to reexamine my passions for my next step as they had faded in the busyness of my life. I had lost the connection of the passions I had as a child.

Tony Robbins, in his book *Awaken The Giant Within*, suggests we take the "job" out of exploring our passions and look at what inspires us. He further suggests asking ourselves what was the first, then the second, and then the third thing we wanted to be when we grew up. Once you do this, you will start to recognize patterns and it facilitates recognition of your passions.

What is something you could do for hours without realizing where the time had gone? What was it that excited us? Gallup suggests one clue to talent, called "Flow" which describes the optimal state of intrinsic motivation. What are you doing when time seems to disappear? Psychologist Nancy Schossberg suggests three ways to research your childhood keepsakes to help you in your next act. Thinking about important things from the past could be valuable to you.

1. **Study yourself as a main character: you, as a child.** Conduct an objective character study. What is the main character's demeanor? Look at photos, diaries, report cards, yearbooks. Are there interests with who you were or to who you are now?

2. **Repurpose:** Childhood photos reveal more about your personality than posed smiley photos. Do your notes or diaries describe your career dreams? What do your report cards show? What interests do you have in common with the character today? What did you abandon that you'd like to reclaim?

3. **Consider repurposing your childhood dreams and passions**. Take characteristics of your childhood dream profession. Volunteer in those areas. For instance, I found photos of myself performing on the stage, singing in the choir, and playing in the band. I have not done those things in many years. How could I transfer that passion now?

Revise your life narrative and adjust to fit your goals You can repurpose your creative focus. For instance, I found creativity in music and the arts as a child. How could I implement that in this stage of life?

Childhood memories stay etched in our minds for a long time. Channeling our childhood positivity and curiosity can rekindle connection with ourselves.

|································|

Explore childhood passions to connect patterns to your adult self.

33. HAPPY MEALS AT HOME

Just remember, it all started with a mouse.

—Leo Busagilia, author

Like many Americans, the thought of the McDonald's Happy Meal evokes a form of happiness—a meal in a box and a treat to go along with it. One of my favorite times as my boys were growing up was to have family dinners together.

I strived to make them "happy meals" and our "treat" was good conversation and getting in touch with each other. Studies show that the family dinner hour creates closer connections. Research has also proven that eating dinner as a family at least five times a week can lower obesity and drug use. At times when family members are going in many directions, you can order a pizza or get take-out food. Make a homemade salad. It does not have to be elaborate. You can use your own dishes for the aesthetic touch.

Now that my boys are young adults, when together we strive to have the "no tv" rule and "put all the cell phones in a basket" rule to increase communication and decrease distractions. In our family, I started assigning each person a role for the dinner hour. Sometimes the task was to set or clean up the table, sometimes to cut the vegetables, or other times to find out what each person wanted to drink and prepare their glasses with their choice. One of my sons loved the job of lighting the candles and selecting the music. He may have been part pyromaniac; however, it was a memorable part of the dinner and kept him engaged. He felt pride in his contribution and his part of the happy meal.

It added to the experience of everyone being a part of it versus all the work being done by me. We also often used the crockpot, where the meal would be waiting for all of us. It's such a pleasure now to have one of my young adult sons call or write for one of those family recipes. A memory was created and is being passed down.

Studies show when families eat together, they tend to eat more vegetables and fruits and less fast food. The National Center on Addiction and Substance Abuse at Columbia University recently reported that eating dinner as a family helped kids in many ways. It helped their progress in school and kept them away from cigarettes and alcohol.

Janet Peterson, in her book *Remedies for the 'I Don't Cook Syndrome,'* says, "Eating dinner together regularly provides more than good nutrition; it enables family members to share their days with each other, relax, laugh, discuss social issues and strengthen family relationships."

Eating together as a family increases family bonding, saves money, is healthier, teaches communication skills, and helps the family appreciate family traditions and connecting as a *family unit*.

|································|

Create your own frequent "Happy Meals"
for deeper family connection.

34. IMPERFECTION AND CONNECTION

The word "imperfect" actually spells "I'm perfect" because everyone is perfect in their own imperfect ways.

—Author Unknown

Dr. Brené Brown, a research professor at the University of Houston, has made her life's work the study of shame and the impact of not feeling "good enough."

Brown calls feeling worthy, connected, loved, and loving souls, "The Wholehearted." Her research shows that what the Wholehearted have is the courage to tell the story of who they are with their whole heart. They have the grace to be imperfect. According to Dr. Brown, the wholehearted are kind to themselves, even when they are imperfect. Connection begins when one is comfortable enough with themselves to be authentic and forge relationships based on who they are—not who they "should" be.

I have found that embracing imperfection and my

vulnerability has allowed me to connect to others more. In sales, we often think we have to say what the customer wants to hear. In a speech, we often prepare thinking that we have to say what the audience is looking for or what someone else has said or believes. In new friendships, sometimes it's hard to be ourselves, thinking we may not be accepted. Giving others a peek at your imperfections often allows greater transparency on their part.

Being encouraged by Brené Brown was empowering for me in these areas of sales, speaking, and friendship. It has enabled greater love and acceptance for myself, a greater comfort level of confidence with friendships, and more vulnerability when giving speeches. It has allowed me to see other's strengths and to become more aware of like-souled people. Leadership requires us to accept imperfection.

It takes awareness of self to accept our own imperfections and offer vulnerability. It has a ripple effect, and we get stronger with time. If you aspire to connect, learn to accept your imperfection and that of others.

"I define connection as the energy that exists between people when they feel seen, heard, and valued; when they can give and receive without judgment; and when they derive sustenance and strength from the relationship," says Brené.

|·······························|

Practice accepting imperfection to enable connection.

35. TRADITIONS

*If there ever comes a day when we can't be together,
keep me in your heart, I'll stay there forever.*

—A.A. Milne, author of *Winnie-the-Pooh*

Today is Christmas Eve and I couldn't help but smile while driving through the neighborhood and surrounding areas. The lights, wreaths, music, and the intangible spirit, all signaling that Christmas was on the way. However, there was greater impact than the realization that a holiday was near. It reminded me that this is the time our communities and country connect on so many levels. After a recent national election where our country was divided, there was something that made me feel all was right with the world once again.

We carry on traditions from our past and begin to make new ones as people and circumstances enter our lives. Tradition brings families and people together, which creates a sense of comfort and familiarity. Our traditions serve as a conduit for our connections.

CONNECTION YOU!

My family started a tradition when my two sons were young of sprinkling "Reindeer dust" on the front lawn. "Reindeer dust" is a combination of glitter, oats, and sugar. After making it, we all gathered as a family in our jammies before bedtime and sprinkled the magic recipe everywhere on the front lawn in preparation of Santa's arrival. After it was sprinkled throughout the yard, the moon helped make it sparkle so Santa and the reindeer could find our home. When Santa is delivering the packages inside, the reindeer eat the oats outside. Although we don't actually make "Reindeer dust" any longer, my sons jokingly comment on Christmas Eve that there is one thing left we need to do before retiring for the evening. This family tradition will most likely be carried on to their families.

Traditions matter for our well-being and not only at the holidays. Rituals can be a bedtime story, a special meal that is symbolic of a special day, having pizza night every Thursday, or waving goodbye to a friend until they are out of sight. It brings warmth, shapes memories, and reminds us we are not alone. Traditions add a certain magic that creates interactions and bonds between us. They allow us to be part of something bigger than ourselves and contribute to a sense of comfort and belonging.

|································|

Reflect on traditions that you could implement to strengthen bonds and connections.

36. QUIETING MY MIND ON THE MAT

Yoga is not about touching your toes. It is what you learn on the way down.

—Jigar Gor, Yoga Doctor

When I discovered yoga, it was one of the first activities that totally calmed me to remove all the outside clutter and thoughts and slow down that busy mind of mine. Yoga literally means "union." It's a union that unites your individual consciousness with a divine consciousness that allows us to quiet our minds and reconnect with ourselves. I cannot seem to do this anywhere completely except on my yoga mat.

Yoga is about harmonizing the body with your mind and breath and offers forms of meditation. I find it my escape for one hour, when I am fully connected to me. There are no phones ringing or outside distractions. There are many physical benefits to yoga:

1. It releases stress.

2. It allows you to create postures and positions that allow you to breathe more freely.

3. It benefits your joints to loosen up and also strengthens your spine.

4. All ages benefit, from children to seniors, and there are a variety of types of yoga to fit all skill levels.

5. Yoga helps your adrenal glands to fight stress and helps lower cortisol levels to help the body deal with anxiety, stress, and depression.

6. Most of the yoga instructors I have experienced stress not to compare yourself to others while you are on your mat and that each class is your own practice. I have embraced that teaching and learned to enjoy the hour as a gift to myself to gain mental clarity, discipline, and the physical benefit of greater flexibility.

You can practice yoga in a private home, in a private session, while watching a DVD or at a studio or gym. There are also websites you can subscribe to if you travel or desire to do a home practice, such as www.gaiam.com. Yoga encourages overall health and wellness and the opportunity to connect to self like no other way I have experienced. Trust me, if you stick with it, try a variety of classes and studios, you will get better and appreciate a new calmness and serenity that truly calms your mind and connects you to yourself.

|································|

Give yoga a try to add calmness and connection to self.

37. MENTORS CONNECT YOU TO SUCCESS

A mentor is someone who allows you to see the hope inside yourself.

—Oprah Winfrey

Everyone can benefit from having a mentor(s). They can give advice, inspiration, and shortcuts. A mentor can help you find new ways of looking at the world and can help hold you accountable to your goals.

Tony Robbins, a number-one life and business strategist, believes in having more than one mentor in your life as learning and training never stops. In a recent training session, he shared with the audience that everyone has different gifts and each role model will teach you something different. He personally has several mentors to assist with his money, physical body, and support as father and husband.

There have been times in my personal life that I needed

extra support with my business, spiritually and physically. Finding mentors helped bring out the best in me. When I did not have the strength or power to change, it was certainly better than standing on the sidelines just wishing.

Mentors can:

1. Help you clarify your goals.

2. Give you honest feedback.

3. Support you after a setback and help you look at your situation in a different light.

4. Motivate and inspire you to take action and help move you forward.

I cherish the mentors in my life who have helped me connect with myself for personal growth. Mentors can also be in the form of books, TED Talks, and audiobooks. We don't have to do it alone.

Implementing mentoring into your life can connect you to your success. You can have more than one mentor; it's "real estate" for your brain and your soul for self-connection.

Who allows you to see the hope inside yourself? A mentor is someone who allows you to know that.

|································|

Add forms of mentoring, people, tapes, and books into your life to connect to your success.

38. SALMON ENCHANTED EVENING

I cook with wine. Sometimes I even add it to the food.

—W.C. Fields, American comedian

Food has the power to transport us to special memories in our life and to connect us to memories and feelings. It also provides an opportunity to share a meal with people to create memories.

I hosted a dinner party for ten friends at my home to celebrate a special occasion. I sent an invitation stating that it would be "A Salmon Enchanted Evening" with good food and good friends. Of course, as you may have guessed, the main course was salmon along with salads, great wine, and dessert. The theme generated excitement.

There is great pleasure and memories when I make memorable meals. Food plays a role in bringing us closer to others. Entertaining is equally about spending quality time with your friends as it is good food. Food is a universal welcome that is about the experience.

In his book *Never Eat Alone and Other Secrets*, Keith Ferrazzi writes about how impactful dinner parties can be to create memories and strengthen relationships. He also states you don't need to worry about being a great chef; you can pick up prepared foods from the grocery store or deli. The author suggests inviting guests that you do not always hang out with so that you can connect to a larger group of friends. This can be very powerful in a social or business setting.

My experience in creating a fun dinner party is to create a theme, provide a warm invitation to my guests, create an appropriate atmosphere with music, flowers, or candles. Placing guests beside someone new enlightens conversation.

An important lesson to remember is you don't have to cook every dish.

If you don't work all day, you can be a more enjoyable hostess. Almost every dinner party in which I entertain is thematic, which is half the enjoyment!

After all, that is the most important connection of all . . . to have fun and create memories.

|································|

Host dinner parties to create new relationships and strengthen your old ones.

39. SIGN, SIGN, EVERYWHERE A SIGN

*People crave comfort, people crave connection,
people crave community.*

—Marianne Williamson, spiritual teacher

The catchy lyrics recorded by the Five Man Electrical Band reminds us that signs are all around us. Signs give us directions and warnings; they express an idea or a command. Stop signs, caution signs, and slowing down for the school bus are signs we see as part of our daily routines that are easily recognized. There are other signs around us that are displayed for public view or advertising that we see; however, we must train ourselves to pay attention, as they are not as routine as the warning signs.

One Saturday morning, a huge cabinet fell off my kitchen wall that stored all my fine china. When I saw all the broken glass, I related to Humpty Dumpty, who sat on a wall and had a great fall. I knew that it could not be put back together again. Off I ventured to my local Home Depot, hoping perhaps to find heavy secure nails or advice. As I sat in the parking lot, I noticed a colorful and happily painted van of a little man holding tools that read, "Handy Man, we fix everything A-Z." Hmm, was this a sign of help?

I used my cell phone to call the number on the truck. When the gentleman answered, I said, "Hello, are you in Home Depot?" "Who is this?" he responded. I then shared I was in the parking lot and saw his truck and conveyed what my dilemma was. He directed me to what aisle he was in, we met in person, and two hours later Humpty Dumpty's helper was putting up my cabinet.

Years later, AZ is still my handyman and has fixed countless things in my home, from faucets and locks to installations. Additionally, many of my friends benefit from his services as I shared his great service and skills.

Paying attention, being aware to looking and listening to signs is a good habit because you never what you may learn or who you may connect with that can aid your situation. Alertness and awareness are often not innate behavior, but with practice you can become more aware of your surroundings and you'll naturally start paying attention and connections will start forming.

Sign, sign, everywhere a sign.

|································|

Train yourself to pay attention to signs around you.

40. STEP INTO CONNECTION

It's a visual world and people respond to visuals.

—Joe Sacco, journalist

My lifelong walking friend, Karol, shared a great way she connected exercise and her relationship. Newly married, she was a runner and her husband a walker. They wanted to connect with their mutual goal of good health via exercise. They began walking daily on a college-walking track.

To help motivate them, they came up with the idea of a creative connection to their walking. They selected a United States map and began to keep track of their mileage and chart it with a thick black line on the map. They wanted to walk the entire United States and begin in her birthplace of San Francisco and walk to Washington, DC.

They would keep track of the daily miles they walked and enter them monthly so they could see their progress on the map. As they traveled the highways from San Francisco to Washington, DC on vacations, they were familiar with the towns, sites, and adventures they had walked.

As they continued their circles around the college walking path, they had a renewed purpose of "walking across America." Each time they would add up their miles, they would see the progress and the places they had "walked by."

The connection of their walking for health and motivation became more enjoyable as the visual black line was extending across map of the United States. As the days, weeks, and months passed. they achieved their goal of walking 2,815 miles.

Creating an activity and charting it visually can be a great way to connect and enhance motivation with a friend or partner with exercise or other related work and home goals. This could be especially helpful and fun for a tedious task or challenged relationship. The journey of 2,815 miles begins with one step.

|······························|

Create a visual for a goal to deepen connection with another person.

41. VISION BOARD

Faith is taking the first step even when you don't see the whole staircase.

—Martin Luther King, Jr., activist

Visualization can accelerate achievement. A vision board is a perfect tool to help you do that. In the book *The Secret*, it states, "The law of attraction is forming your entire life experience and it is doing that through your thoughts. When you are visualizing, you are emitting a powerful frequency out into the Universe."

Vision boards are tangible boards or notebooks that represent your goals and dreams. They are built with collages of words and pictures from magazines or the computer or your own photos. I have also used cards received or brochures collected. The goal is to look at them daily to stimulate your emotions, as our minds respond strongly to visual stimulation.

"A picture is worth a thousand words" became true for me. It has attracted me to places, things, and people as it has helped me visualize what I want to bring in my life. It is a daily reminder and has become part of my self conscious. It has been a constant reminder of what I want to attract in my life. Also, having something to strive for with visuals has added optimism as well as create a greater vibration around me.

When I trained with Jack Canfield, success coach and founder of Chicken Soup for the Soul, he outlined a six-step process for making vision boards:

1. Create a list of goals you'd like to achieve in the next year.

2. Collect a bundle of magazines, newspapers, whatever media might speak to you.

3. Find pictures that represent your goals and inspire you.

4. Make a collage out of your collected photos.

5. Add motivational "affirmation words" that represent how you want to feel.

6. Contemplate your vision board every day.

Feel and see yourself daily with your vision board. Build your vision board to what you want to become and attract in your life.

|································|

Create a vision board to connect to your goals and dreams.

42. GRATITUDE JOURNAL

If we magnified blessings as much as we magnify disappointments, we would all be much happier.

—John Wooden, basketball coach

I was inspired to start a gratitude journal. I keep it on my nightstand, and I jot down what I am thankful on most days before I go to sleep. I selected one with a beautiful cover and looking at it reminds me that I have much to be thankful for. It has been a ritual that brings me peace each night before going to bed. It has now become a habit and when looking back over the entries, makes me smile, brings me joy and I have connected to myself on deeper levels.

My gratitude journal has helped me with:

1. Lower stress levels, knowing I have good in my life.

2. A sense of calm before bed.

3. Focusing on what really matters instead of worrying about what is wrong.

4. On days when I feel blue, reflecting back helps me remember that I have great people and things in my life.

5. Gaining clarity on what is really important.

6. Writing has increased my optimism to realize how rich my life really is.

Sheryl Sandberg, COO of Facebook, lost her husband of many years to a sudden heart attack. In her commencement address to the University of California at Berkeley, she shared that her Rabbi gave her great advice to help her during the grieving process. He encouraged her to write down three moments of joy before going to bed each night. She shared that it had changed her life because she was able to go to bed thinking of something cheerful.

Gratitude is a powerful mindset for attracting what we want and the people we want to keep and draw into our lives. It allows us to continually look for things to appreciate in our lives.

|································|

Start a gratitude journal to attract positive vibrations into your life.

43. EMOTIONAL INTELLIGENCE

No one cares how much you know, until they know how much you care.

—Theodore Roosevelt, 26th president of the United States

Emotional intelligence refers to the ability to identify and manage one's own emotions, as well as the emotions of others. It is about learning to operate from a place of wisdom, skill, and emotional intelligence ("emotional quotient," or "EQ" as it's sometimes known).

In his book *Working With Emotional Intelligence*, Daniel Goleman lists the components that identify the four different levels of emotional intelligence to manage emotions.

1. **Perceiving emotions:** The first step in understanding emotions is to perceive them accurately. In many cases, this might involve understanding nonverbal signals such as facial expressions and body language.

2. **Reasoning with emotions:** The next step involves using emotions to promote thinking and cognitive activity. Emotions help prioritize what we pay attention and react to; we respond emotionally to things that garner our attention.

3. **Understanding emotions:** Emotions we perceive can carry a wide variety of meanings. What do we observe from a person's anger?

4. **Managing emotions:** The ability to manage emotions is an important part of emotional intelligence and emotional management.

EQ is a great way to discover more about ourselves and take action. Along with self-awareness, listening to feedback and paying attention to the four-step process will provide professional and personal growth.

Understanding emotions can be the key to better relationships and improved well-being.

|······························|

Select one element of EQ that would enhance your life if you paid more attention to it.

44. OWNING YOUR POWER

"Take the power to make your life happy."
—Susan Polis Schutz, American poet

I have thought a great deal in the last two years about owning my power after events occurred that triggered me toward a journey of discovering my own power. Shifting our internal language is powerful. It has made a significant difference in my happiness and confidence. We can all learn to do this.

When I see myself as weak and indecisive, I tell myself I am brave and confident. I often read daily affirmations to reinforce this self-talk.

There have been times in my life that I thought my voice did not matter or that I wasn't as smart as someone else or I didn't have the family background that allowed me to do certain things. Now I speak up more and express my opinions, knowing that perhaps my voice could make a difference in someone's life.

As I kept track of some of my negative thoughts, I realized they were not serving me in personal growth or being my best self. In fact, they were harming me. Some of my beliefs came from other people. I now focus more conscientiously on my own thoughts and using my personal gifts without explanation or regret.

I also made a shift in the way I view friendships. A wise friend recently shared with me that there is a difference in those who support you and those who enrich your life. New connections in our lives can provide growth and the ability to think in new directions. There are some friendships that we occasionally need to shed in order to move forward or set new boundaries.

I seek support from friends and they seek support from me. It's important to reach out to check in and know we are not alone. In connecting to ourselves on a deeper level, we need to find out what and who brings us down and who can lift us up. Finding the inner voice that can lift us up adds to our personal growth, wellness, and happiness. It enables us to put our best to the world when we learn to own our power.

⊢∙∙∙∙∙∙∙∙∙∙∙∙∙∙∙∙∙∙∙∙∙∙∙∙∙∙∙∙⊣

Seek ways to discover your own personal power
for personal connection.

45. SECRETS TO CREATIVITY

Don't underestimate the value of doing nothing,
of just going along, listening to all the things you
can't hear, and not bothering.

—Joan Powers, *Pooh's Little Instruction Book*

I must admit, I am a task-oriented person. Likewise, I am told over and over from those close to me that I am one of the most creative people they have met. I will take that as a compliment for the most part, because I do have a busy mind that loves to create. I get great self-satisfaction from creating. However, when I do slow down and just "be," my mind creates more, which provides a bank of creative activity for the future.

Here are some things I do to ignite my creativity:

1. **Walk**—my favorite exercise. Sometimes I just walk and absorb nature. I find new trails or walk cities when I travel. Additionally, I listen to my recorded books on Audible. Either way, walking helps me create and I get dual benefit from the exercise. I keep

my iPhone close and use the Notes App to record my ideas if something exciting comes to me that I might forget.

2. **Bookstore**—I love spending time in a bookstore. I have several favorite aisles that I frequent. I find books and authors I have never heard of and enjoy sitting on the floor, skimming and reading. Often, new ideas spark. I take notes all the time. I organize my Notes app with topics such as books to read, quotes I like, movies to see, things to investigate. The hours pass so quickly for me in a bookstore, and I come out with a year full of ideas.

I believe creativity doesn't come from any one activity. It comes from a variety of sources when I am relaxing, having fun, or being in stillness. I consider these activities self-care and part of my well-being plan. Friends have shared they get creative when they watch movies, do a craft, ride bikes, etc. The list is endless.

Don't underestimate the value of down time and the opportunity to recharge your creativity by being in a new environment or around new people. Seeds of creativity can be planted, followed by peacefulness, excitement, and joy, which all allow for deeper connection with yourself.

|································|

Make time to let your creative juices
flow in activities you enjoy.

REFLECTIONS ON CONNECTING WITH SELF

1. What are some activities that bring you joy, peace, and energy? (Keep these experiences close, when in need of alone time,) Try to list ten.

_____

_____

_____

_____

_____

_____

_____

_____

_____

_____

_____

2. Start a list of activities or hobbies that you would like to do as time and resources become available.

_____

_____

_____

_____

_____

_____

_____

_____

_____

3. What are activities that you dislike doing and would like to do less of? Try to list ten.

_____

_____

_____

_____

_____

_____

_____

_____

_____

_____

4. Look at this list and consider if there are any of these activities that you can remove from your life or shift to another person.

_____

_____

_____

_____

_____

_____

_____

_____

_____

5. Consider your five senses of taste, sight, smell, touch, and hearing. Think about the ones that have the most impact on you. What memories come to mind? The idea is to think about which of our senses lift us to a happier state and to allow ourselves to put more in our lives to be more fully alive.

_____

_____

_____

_____

_____

_____

_____

_____

CONNECTION YOU!

SMELL—What is a smell that makes you happy? Why?

TASTE—Choose one meal a week where you slow down and think about all the tastes with that meal. Salty? Sweet? Did you enjoy the meal more?

Touch—Practice awareness of what touches your body. Think about the power of hugs and how often you give or receive.

SIGHT—Close your eyes and imagine "seeing" a place that brings you happiness. Make a goal to "see" things you have not noticed before without purposely observing. Pay attention to how your body is feeling. Consider writing your thoughts down.

SOUND—Practice closing your ears and taking in all the sounds around you. What do you hear? Consider doing this exercise several times a week to focus on what is around you.

6. What do you know about your family tree?

7. When is a time in your life when you felt lonely?

8. When is a time you spoke to a cashier at a store or a person at an airport who you did not know? Did it make a difference?

9. What was your favorite story in this section? Why?

10. Consider one thing that you will do new for yourself. Make a goal to incorporate that change for a period of time; write the date and look at it one month from today.

CONNECTING WITH SELF ACTION LIST

- **Try meditation**—Try adding five to ten minutes of meditation to your day. Meditation can help you visualize things and help put aside distractions for a period of time. My meditation practice has increased my self-awareness, positivity, and energy.

- **Increase exercise**—It can help make you look better, feel stronger, reduce stress, and gain a sense of accomplishment. Once this becomes routine for you, it may increase connectivity with others. (Exercise can help in several forms of addiction recovery as well.)

- **Resources**—Local gyms and community centers in your area are great resources or put on your tennis shoes, open your door, and take a walk!

- **Create a gratitude journal**—Creating a gratitude journal can give you greater control of your thoughts and feelings. It can move your thinking from what is right with your life versus what is wrong. Gratitude is correlated with optimism. It can take less than five minutes a day and create a habit of noticing grateful moments. Journals can be purchased or simply use an inexpensive notebook.

- **Set specific "me" time**—Put yourself on the calendar. Consider what fills you with joy and time flows. It could be baths, sunsets, books, or painting. Make a list and try to have "me time" several times a week. This also involves analyzing how many commitments you are making.

- **Practice self-compassion**—By implementing self-compassion, you learn to treat yourself like a good friend and have less self-criticism. Some of the benefits are better health, better relationships with other people, and less anxiety. Author Kristen Neff offers the three elements of self-compassion : 1.) Self kindness versus self-judgment, 2.) common humanity versus isolation, and 3.) Mindfulness versus over-identification.

  Resource: *The Proven Power of Being Kind To Yourself* by Kristen Neff, Phd

- **Listen to audiobooks**—Listening to books online allows you to engage differently than print. It can allow you to learn a new hobby or listen to a fiction book of interest. It can be a great way to connect to your passions and grow. Audiobooks are great to listen to when you are walking, exercising, or doing chores.

Resource: http://www.audible.com/

- **Implement affirmations**—Buddha says, "What we think we become." Affirmations break patterns of negative thoughts and actions. They raise levels of "positive thought" and can give you the feeling that exercise does. "Affirmation" means to make steady and strengthen. It can be helpful to write your affirmations on index cards in places you see regularly throughout your day.

Resources: http://jackcanfield.com/success/op/affirmations-for-success.html

http://www.louisehay.com/affirmation

RESOURCES

100 Ways to Connect with Self, in Life, and at Work

1. Start your day with meditation.

2. Get up early and to do some type of exercise.

3. Keep a gratitude journal.

4. Walk through a bookstore for creative stimulation.

5. Scan newspaper headlines for a new thoughts.

6. Write a thank-you letter to someone from the past.

7. Take a walk in nature.

8. Visit a national monument or park.

9. Organize a neighborhood barbeque.

10. Check your library bulletin board for new ideas.

11. View bulletin boards of coffee shops for people and places.

12. Volunteer for something you want to learn more about.

13. Walk a mall before it opens and observe the store windows.

14. Organize a theme party such as "Think Like a Cheetah" with participants wearing animal prints or a suggested color.

15. Visit your grocery store and challenge yourself to engage with one employee.

16. Challenge yourself to find one way to substitute something you do with technology to human interaction.

17. Share your smile and be cognizant of the reactions of others.

18. Learn a few nonverbal body language movements.

19. Send someone an e-card.

20. Research a new restaurant to try.

21. Organize a "Come as You Will Be" party to imagine where your coworkers or friends want to be in five years.

22. Find a way to serve.

23. Acknowledge something positive about your past and tie it to something in your present.

24. Create a victory log.

25. Consider hiring a professional organizer for your home.

26. Read the ads in the back of a magazine.

27. Scan the want ads in the newspaper.

RESOURCES

28. Find one person in your yearbook to reconnect with and discover what they are doing.

29. Join an online fitness group.

30. Pick a habit to work on developing this next month.

31. Take the CliftonStrengths Assessment to discover your top five talents.

32. Buy coffee for someone behind you in line.

33. Play music that is uplifting and observe your new thought patterns.

34. Organize a board game night with no technology.

35. Go bowling.

36. Enroll in a class that intrigues you.

37. Have a dinner party with new acquaintances.

38. Investigate options for community biking to explore a city or meet new people.

39. Join a book club.

40. Find a business association to join.

41. Go to a cultural event.

42. Try a Toastmasters meeting.

43. Look for an improv group to view or join.

44. Take a dance class.

45. Attend a book signing.

46. Take your book or computer to a coffee shop.

47. Investigate museums in your area.

48. Visit your local farmer's market and ask questions about the organics.

49. Try public transportation.

50. Try doing something alone that you usually do with another person.

51. Say yes to something new.

52. Take a cooking class.

53. Create a "staycation" in your own city and book something new each day.

54. Formulate a "listening" day for work or home to hone your listening skills.

55. Sit on a park bench and observe.

56. Give three compliments today that you have not given this year.

57. Think about someone to express appreciation to at work.

58. Surf the Internet for "free things to do in your city."

59. Check out Ultimate Frisbee!

60. Check out local college and university activities for the community.

61. Play upbeat music before an appointment to put you in a new mood.

62. Challenge yourself to begin sentences with only positive vibes, and take out "not."

63. Launch a blog.

64. Ask for help on something you want to learn or need to accomplish.

65. Start a collection.

66. Indulge in a modest splurge.

67. Master a new technology.

68. Find someone to draw stick figures with to create a dialogue.

69. Give a positive review of something you purchased online.

70. Consider whom you could throw a celebration for.

71. Buy pens with a positive message and distribute them to coworkers.

72. Organize a movie night.

73. Create a pizza night and have everyone bring a favorite ingredient.

74. Invite a speaker to your workplace for group stimulation.

75. Have a "knock-knock " joke day at work. Consider a bulletin board for posting.

76. Write your five senses down on paper and enjoy each in one new way today.

77. Organize an event and ask five people to bring one new person to it.

78. Find a mentor. Consider churches, libraries, Score, and the government for resources.

79. Pay a sincere compliment to someone.

80. Check out your local zoo.

81. Go to a parade and observe the sidelines.

82. Consider a way you could become involved in local politics.

83. Start paying attention to flyers and bulletin boards.

84. Wear remarkable socks or ties.

85. Join a Supper Club.

86. Have a "temporary tattoo" party or day at the office. This creates terrific conversation.

87. Check out your local chamber of commerce.

88. Volunteer at a community race with registration or handing out water.

89. Listen to a podcast.

90. Organize a scavenger hunt for the office or neighborhood.

91. Boost morale in the office by taking song requests and blast them on the PA system on Friday.

92. Ban emails for a day and encourage personal interactions for one day in the office.

93. Start an office design committee to spruce up aesthetics within your office.

94. Have a "show and tell" in your office to share and learn new ideas.

95. Create a "lottery ticket" jar; put names during the week for accomplishments and draw at the end of the week.

96. Take a walk in a public place and say hello to everyone you pass.

97. Put a funny sticker on someone's back in the office and watch the connection in your office.

98. Get to know the family of friends and coworkers by having an event at work or in the community and encourage people to bring a family member.

99. Test-drive a sports car.

100. Start a "ta da" list of cool things you have done and add to it each day.

MY CONNECTION
COMMITMENT

I commit to the following to increase my connections to others and myself for greater happiness and well-being:

_____

_____

_____

_____

_____

_____

_____

_____

_____

_____

_____

ACKNOWLEDGEMENTS AND ANGEL-KNOWLEDGEMENTS

I was first encouraged to write a book from a friend who had heard me speak and thought I had a lot to say. Self-talk said, *"Wow, an author, me?"* I believe we get divine intervention from the voices of others.

Spencer and Max, I hope you'll embrace these stories and consider your own meaningful connections that will lead to a fulfilled life with others and within yourselves. You both have so much to offer to the world. I hope you will be encouraged to share your gifts and be bold in doing so. I am so proud of your sensitivity and amazing hearts. You are the two most important connections in my life. I am so proud of you and for being two amazing human beings. I will always remain connected to you as you are woven in my heart.

Angels are spiritual beings believed to act as an attendant, agent, guardian, or messenger represented in human form. An angel is a caring person. They show you love and compassion and sometimes appear when you need it the most.

During the writing of this book, I had a surprise sudden disconnection in my life in which I had no warning to prepare. It was devastating to me and life became overwhelming, which caused temporary disconnection from life slowed the writing of this book. I found one of the fastest ways back to self-connection was through other people offering support and encouragement. I am grateful to the following angels who supported me on many levels to reconnect to who I was and helping reattach my wings to fly again.

Thank-you to: *Donna Beard, Ramona and George Brandt, Jennifer Bennett, Nansea Bright, Lori Clarke, Cindy Fleming, Susan Fuchs, Karol Harris, Annette Lawlor, Pat and Jeff James, Tracy Key, Darleen Knapp, Dayna Kuhar, Kathy Lindstedt, Debbie Meadows, Nicole Monroe, Marsha Nelms Muawwad, ML and Greg Murray, Cindy Ramsdell, Donna Ritter, Marilyn Rose, Lori Rowen, Dawn Sanok, Michelle Sterne, and Katherine Wood.*

I also thank all the strangers I met who offered me a smile and friendly words on days when I needed them most. I hope to daily "pay it back." You never know when you can influence another's life by saying hello or offering a smile. Connection matters.

I am most grateful to Capital Speakers Club of Washington, DC, and the mentorship of Dr. Jean Miller, who has assisted me in learning the principles of connecting with an audience while public speaking.

I am convinced that I was given the gift of inspiration and connection as a superpower. I can help others and businesses learn how to be mindful and how to connect with other people. Learning to connect with others can change your life, others' lives, and most importantly, save lives.

How you do anything is how you do everything.

ABOUT THE AUTHOR

Sheila K. Stabile

Sheila K. Stabile is the founder of *Connection You*. She speaks, coaches, facilitates, and provides creative insight and leadership development for a wide variety of businesses and organizations.

Prior to founding *Connection You*, Sheila was an educator, award-winning national sales executive, and business development manager for Fortune 500 companies. In 2019, she was elected the 69th President of the Capital Speakers Club of Washington, DC.

Sheila is a Gallup-Certified Strengths Coach© and Jack Canfield Success Principal Trainer©.

She now resides in the Washington, DC metropolitan area. She has two adult sons and is a first-time author.

WHAT'S NEXT?

I would love to continue helping you finding ways to connect to yourself, others, and in business. Please sign up to receive future tips at www.connectionyou.com

You will continue to learn, get tips, challenges, inspiration, and we can personalize a program for you and your company.

- Inspiring Connection Stories
- Happiness Insights
- Connection Practices
- Business Development

If you would like to work with my team, you will find ways to reach out to us on our website. We would love to hear from you.

CONNECTION YOU

Connect with Sheila at www.connectionyou.com and on twitter @SheilaKStabile

CORPORATE WORSHOPS
CONNECTION WORKSHOP

Does your organization need more connections and innovative ways to connect to employees or your customers?

I love working with corporate teams and giving keynotes around intentional connection.

Workshops include topics on how to be more intentional about cultivating connection. With intentional connection, you can learn to be happier and more productive.

STRENGTHSFINDER
TEAM WORKSHOP

An interactive StrengthsFinder workshop is an excellent developmental program for your organization. Sheila Stabile is a Gallup-Certified Strengthsfinder Coach and can facilitate workshops to assist your team in unlocking their talents and intregrate them in their roles for greater connection and team engagement.

CONNECTION YOU!

Some of the takeaways from this workshop are:

- Gain greater self-awareness and team alignment
- Increase employee engagement and business productivity
- Gain techniques to address team challenges
- Understand how to build effective team partnerships
- Transform relationships in the workplace
- Increase individual and team performance
- Use strengths to improve results and reach goals
- Experience an energizing and fun session

KEYNOTE SPEAKING

I am available for keynote speaking engagements and training teams. Please find the keynote request form on my website.

Made in the USA
Columbia, SC
04 February 2020

87267693R00114